Old Mardale

Neil Honeyman

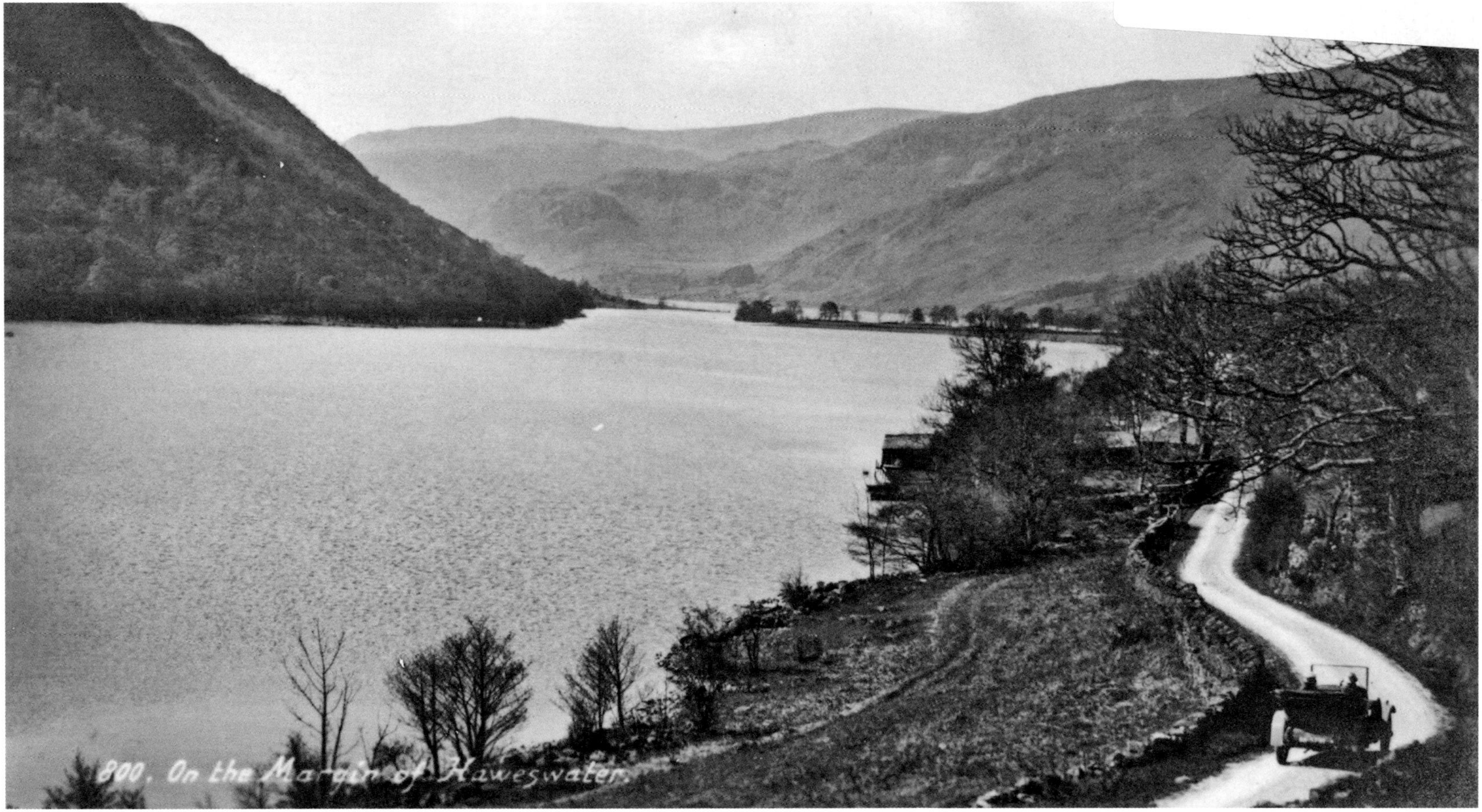

This view, taken from the north, shows an old car making its way along the original road on the west shore of the lake. The Straits, a narrow stretch of water which divided Low Water from High Water, is in the distance. Before the flooding, a new road was constructed on the Naddle side of the lake.

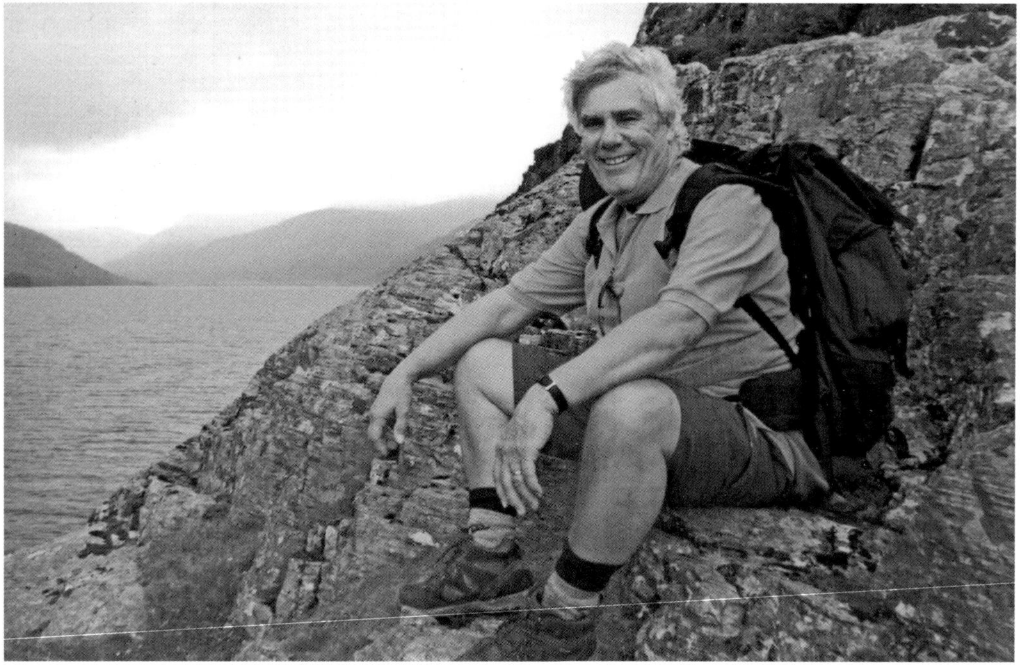

First published in the United Kingdom, 2013,
by Stenlake Publishing Ltd.
01290 551122
www.stenlake.co.uk
ISBN 978-1-84033-639-9

Enjoy!

Neil Honeyman

The author relaxing on the Coast to Coast Walk, July 2012.

Further Reading

The books listed below were used by the author during his research. None are available from Stenlake Publishing; please contact your local bookshop or reference library.

A Backwater In Lakeland, by Isaac Hinchcliffe (1922). A nostalgic look back at a Mardale newly-threatened by Manchester's plans for the valley. The book contains lovely descriptions of the natural beauty of the valley, and a range of interesting photographs.

Mardale, The Drowned Village, by David & Joan Hay (1976). Based on childhood memories of holidays in Mardale during the First World War, this is a fascinating description of a vanished world. Well-illustrated with postcard views and family photgraphs.

Mardale Revisited, by Geoffrey Berry (1984). This book surveys "old" Mardale and describes the impact of the second drought year on the valley. Old and contemporary photographs add to the interest.

The Lost Village Of Mardale, by W.R. Mitchell (1993). Drawing on contemporary sources and Mardalian memories, this book evokes the pastoral life of the valley and the impact of the reservoir project. The book contains a range of interesting photographs and sketches.

A Cast Iron Community, Bampton and District Local History Society (2006). Exhaustive survey of the dam project and the creation and development of the Burnbanks community. A wealth of eye-witness accounts and contemporary photographs are used in the book.

Mardale, Echoes and Reflections of a lost Lakeland community, Shap Local History Society (2011). This recent publication gives the reader highly-detailed descriptions of former inhabitants and buildings in Mardale valley. There are many excellent photographs, some of which I would love to have in my collection!

Introduction

In July 2012 my brother and I completed the Coast-to-Coast Walk, from St.Bees on the Cumbrian coast to Robin Hood's Bay near Whitby. Our father had recently passed away and, as he had also completed it in 2006 at the age of 83, Ian and I decided to repeat the feat in his memory. As we trudged along High Street, high above Haweswater Reservoir, I hoped to catch a glimpse of the remains of old Mardale village which lay beneath the waters, but it was a misty morning and the summer weather had been too wet, so there was nothing to be seen.

Thousands of visitors flock to the Lake District each year. It seems inconceivable that one of its valleys should have been transformed and one of its communities - albeit a tiny one of forty or so souls - should have been evacuated and its homes destroyed, in order to improve Manchester's water supply. Yet all of this happened as recently as the 1930s. Since then only in times of severe drought has the skeleton of Mardale risen from its watery grave.

I have been interested in the Mardale area for many years, even though I have lived for most of my life in or around Barrow-in-Furness, 50 miles away on the South Cumbrian coast. Like many other people, I always keep my eye on the spring and early summer weather in the hope that a prolonged dry spell will lower the reservoir level sufficiently to expose the remains of Mardale once more. Thousands of sightseers will converge on the valley again to examine the foundations of former buildings and walk along the old lanes. Perhaps it is better that we have our wetter summers, as structures such as Chapel Bridge may not survive another tourist invasion.

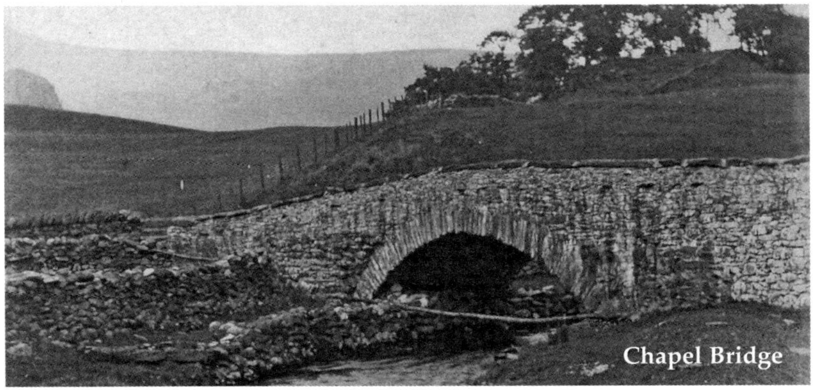
Chapel Bridge

For many years I have been interested in old postcards and photographs, and my aim in writing this book is to examine the record of Mardale left for posterity by the commercial photographers of the last century. Picture postcards were first used in Britain in 1900, but by the 1970s their heyday was long gone, yet this period conveniently encompasses the final years of the Mardale community, the evacuation and subsequent flooding, and the first drought year. National postcard producers such as Raphael Tuck and Valentine's of Dundee largely ignored the Mardale Valley and we are therefore left with a group of Lakeland photographers to keep the memory of old Mardale alive. These include Reed's of Penrith, the Abraham brothers and Pettitt of Keswick, Lowe of Patterdale, Simcoe and Atkinson & Pollitt of Kendal, plus a Burnley photographer called Richard Broughton. Their work provides the bulk of the illustrations in this book.

Collecting postcards of the Mardale Valley can be a rather frustrating hobby! Early photographers wanted to sell their cards, and there was little of interest to the average tourist who might stray into the area. Holy Trinity Church and the Dun Bull Hotel were the more interesting buildings, but most of the cards produced simply show views of the lake or the surrounding hills. I have over 200 cards in my Mardale collection and the majority of them are variations on the above. There were several farms in the Mardale Valley, together with a school and a large vicarage, but it is very difficult to find close-up views of any of them. The same is true of social events, such as the Shepherds' Meets at the Dun Bull Hotel, or of the construction of the Dam and Burnbanks. I am sure that some of these cards must be in family collections. If you have any unusual cards for sale, then I am always interested! Please contact me - varykino@hotmail.co.uk.

I am indebted to the many people who have helped to build up my collection over the years, and to those who have provided assistance in producing this book. I would like to mention collector extraordinaire George Dawson of Kendal, who has been a second father to me for the past 35 years; the late Jane Chambers of Lindale; Clive Torrens of Leyburn; the late John Marsh of Kendal; postcard dealers, past and present; my brother Ian, for walking with me in Mardale and who got me through the Coast-to-Coast Walk; and last but not least, my wife Sylvia who has patiently supported me in my long searches for new material. Most of the illustrations are from postcards in my own collection. The errors - and I am sure that there will be some - are mine also, and I should be happy to be corrected.

The Haweswater Reservoir is now owned by United Utilities PLC and supplies about 25% of the north-west's water supplies. The RSPB maintains a viewing platform in Riggindale Valley, where a lonely male golden eagle awaits a new partner. Since 2012 the society has controlled large areas of woodland on the Naddle side of the valley. Haweswater is the most easterly of the lakes in the Lake District National Park. For most of the year, Mardale is still a quiet and remote valley, unknown to the majority of the tourists who arrive in Cumbria to enjoy the "hotspots" in the Central Lakes - Keswick, Wordsworth's Grasmere, the Beatrix Potter trail, and Ambleside and Bowness on Lake Windermere. There is so much to see and do in the Lake District, and so many places to stay, that Mardale and Haweswater are largely overlooked. Nevertheless, it is a beautiful area, with a great variety of hilltop walks and an abundance of wildlife.

I love visiting Mardale, but my visits are always tinged with sadness. Through my postcard collection and wider reading, I feel that I know the little community that once existed in the valley - and now it is lost forever. Perhaps I am being over-sentimental: the last baptisms took place in Holy Trinity Church and the last drinks were served in the Dun Bull in 1935, some 78 years ago, so there can only be a handful of elderly people with any memory of the "old" Mardale. I'm not one of them, but I'll probably still feel a little sad the next time I visit the valley, and recall these lines from A.E. Housman's "A Shropshire Lad":

Into my heart an air that kills
From yon far country blows:
What are those blue-remembered hills,
What spires, what farms are those?

That is the land of lost content,
I see it shining plain,
The happy highways where I went
And cannot come again.

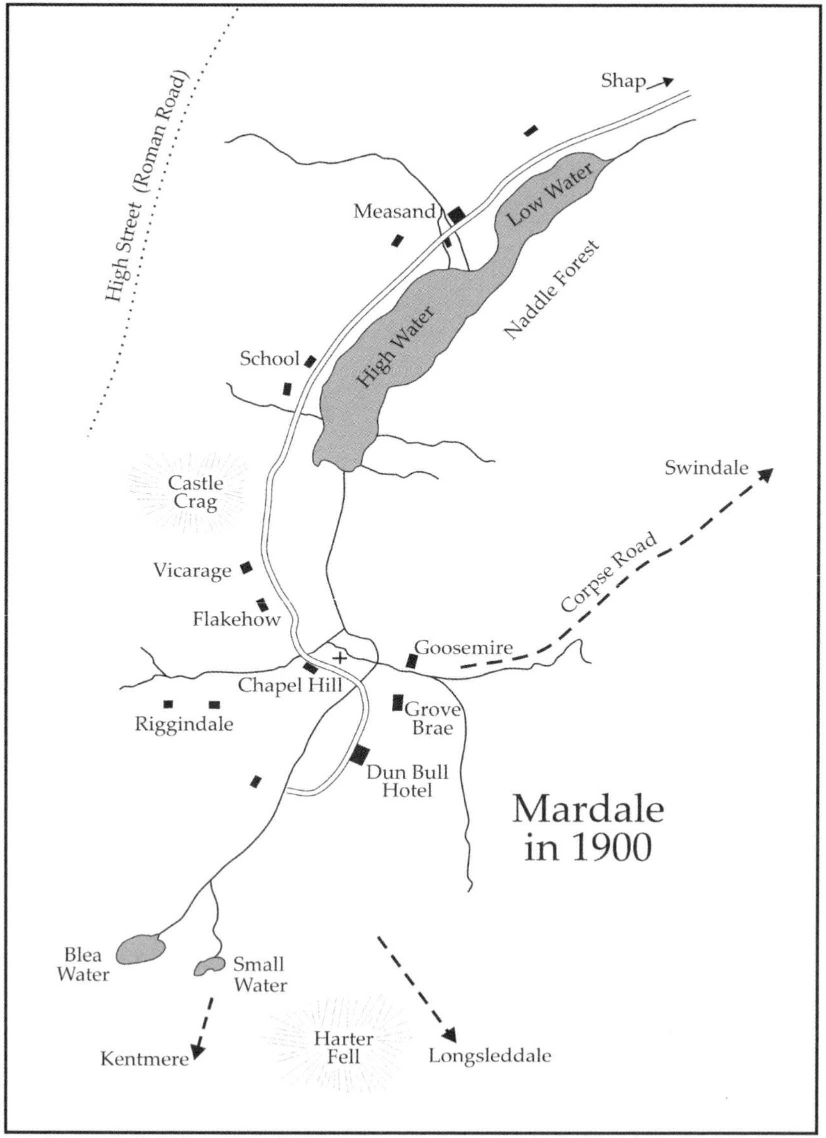

Mardale in 1900.

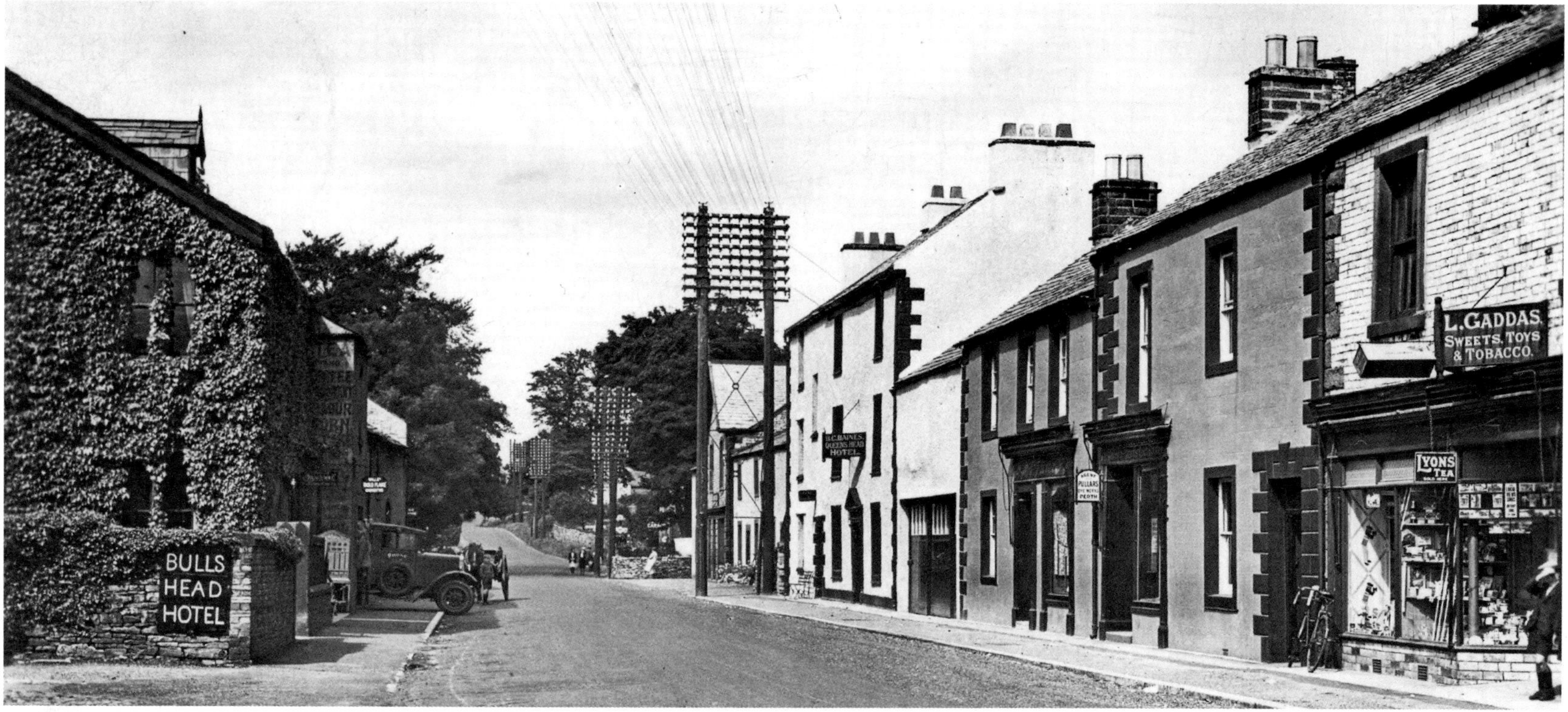

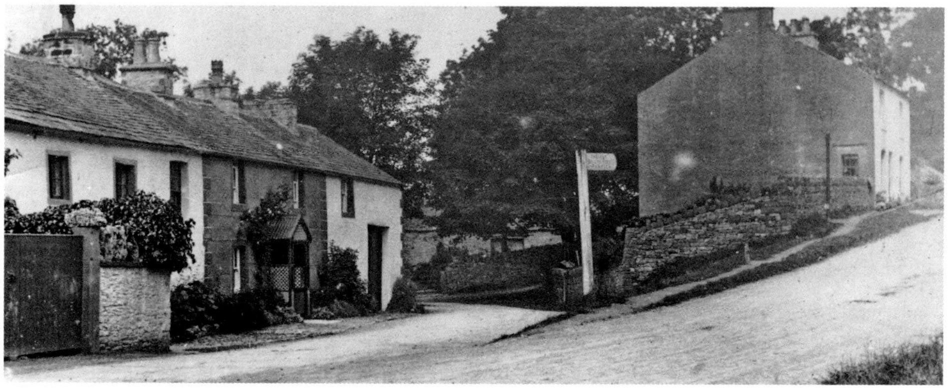

At the turn of the last century, Mardale and Haweswater were in Lakeland's remotest valley: "a backwater in Lakeland", as Isaac Hinchcliffe recorded. There were no direct roads linking the area to the popular tourist destinations in central Lakeland - Bowness, Ambleside, Grasmere and Keswick - and, in fact, the average tourist would have found little of interest in a hamlet with no shops and in a lake with no steamers. The easiest access to the valley was via the A6 road between Kendal and Penrith, turning off at the village of Shap. Visitors could at least have bought provisions there, and possibly have obtained transport to Mardale.

This left turn at the northern end of Shap village would take the traveller to Mardale.

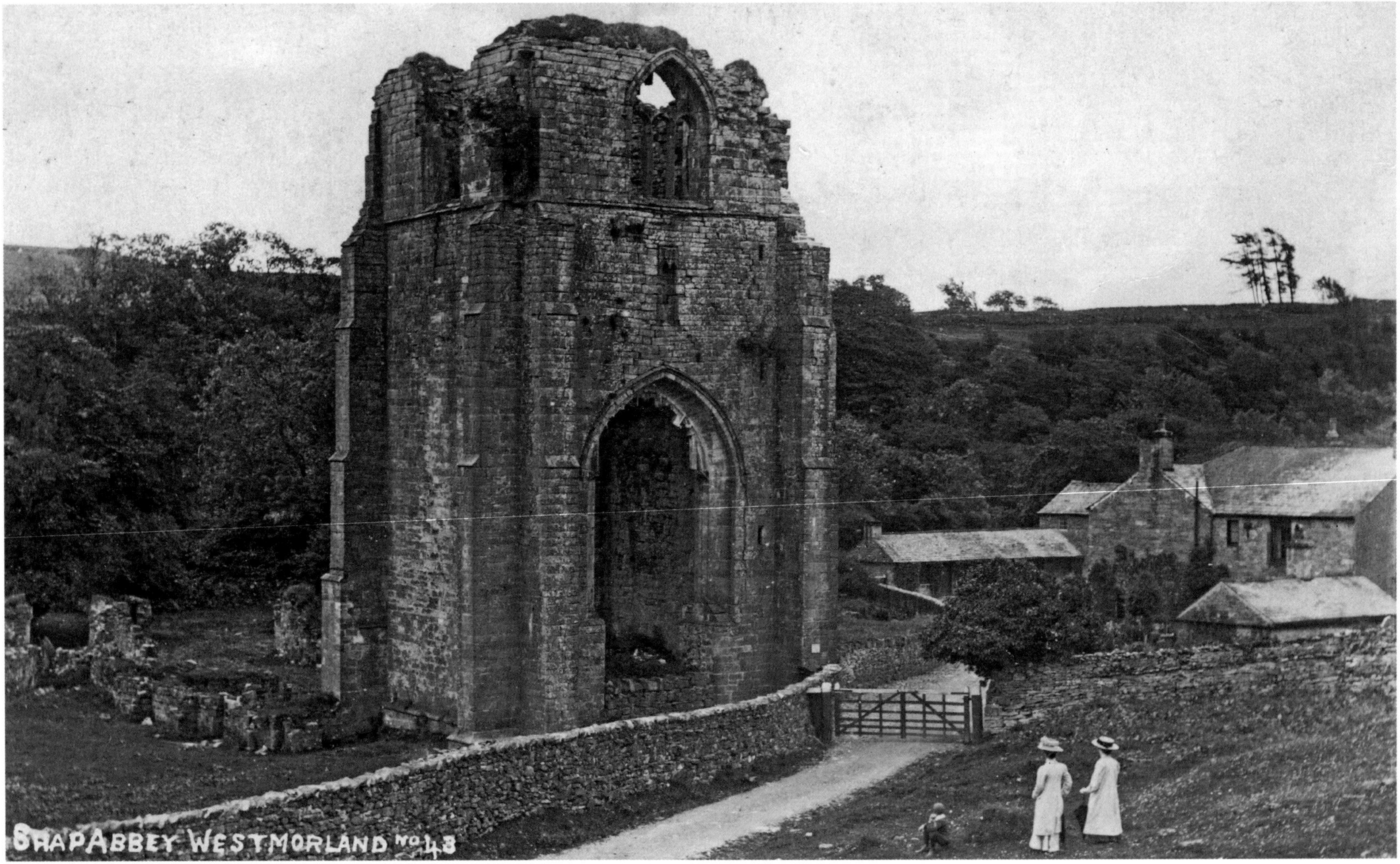

About a mile to the west of Shap the picturesque ruins of Shap Abbey lie beside the River Lowther. The abbey, the last to be established in England, was founded by the Premonstratensians - the White Canons - around 1199. Today, little remains of the abbey. Most of the visible foundations date back to the 13th century, but the impressive tower was built at the beginning of the 16th century. Shap Abbey was the last to be closed during the reign of Henry VIII. Since 1540 much of its stonework has found its way into the fabric of local farms, Shap Market Hall and Lowther Castle.

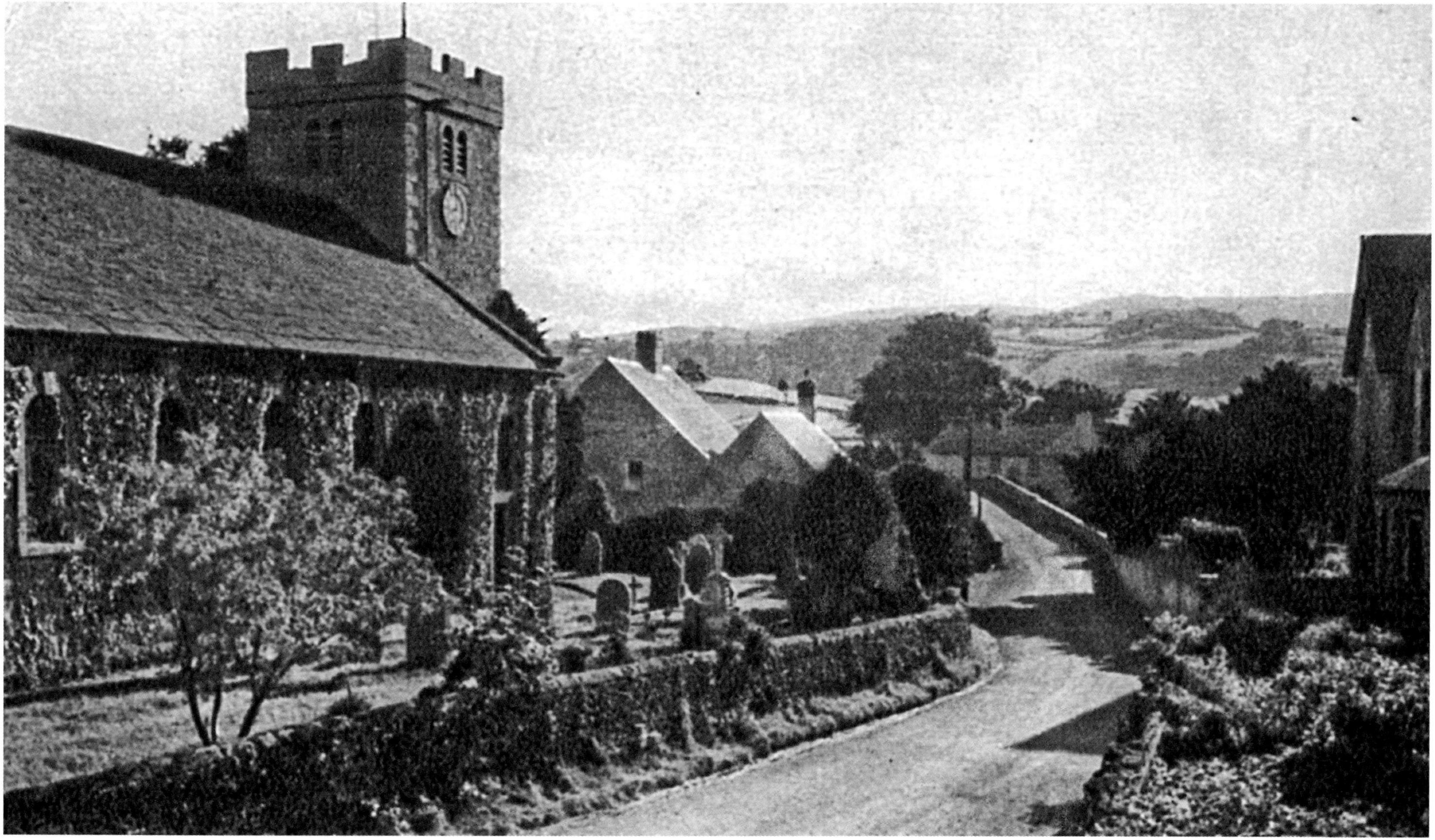

The road routes to Mardale from Penrith (15 miles) and Shap (11 miles) converge at Bampton. This old parish was well-known for its school, which, like Mardale, was very isolated, yet produced a long line of distinguished men. Amongst these was an archbishop of Dublin and chancellor of Ireland, a Bishop of London, and a vice-admiral, plus over 200 priests. The school's religious fame was such that it was said "they drove the plough in Latin in Bampton." Visitors to the area could find refreshment at the St.Patrick's Well Inn at Bampton, or could stay at the Crown and Mitre Hotel at nearby Bampton Grange. St. Patrick's Church, built on an earlier site in 1726, stands at Bampton Grange, and opposite is the Tinklar Library, which houses a large quantity of books in Latin.

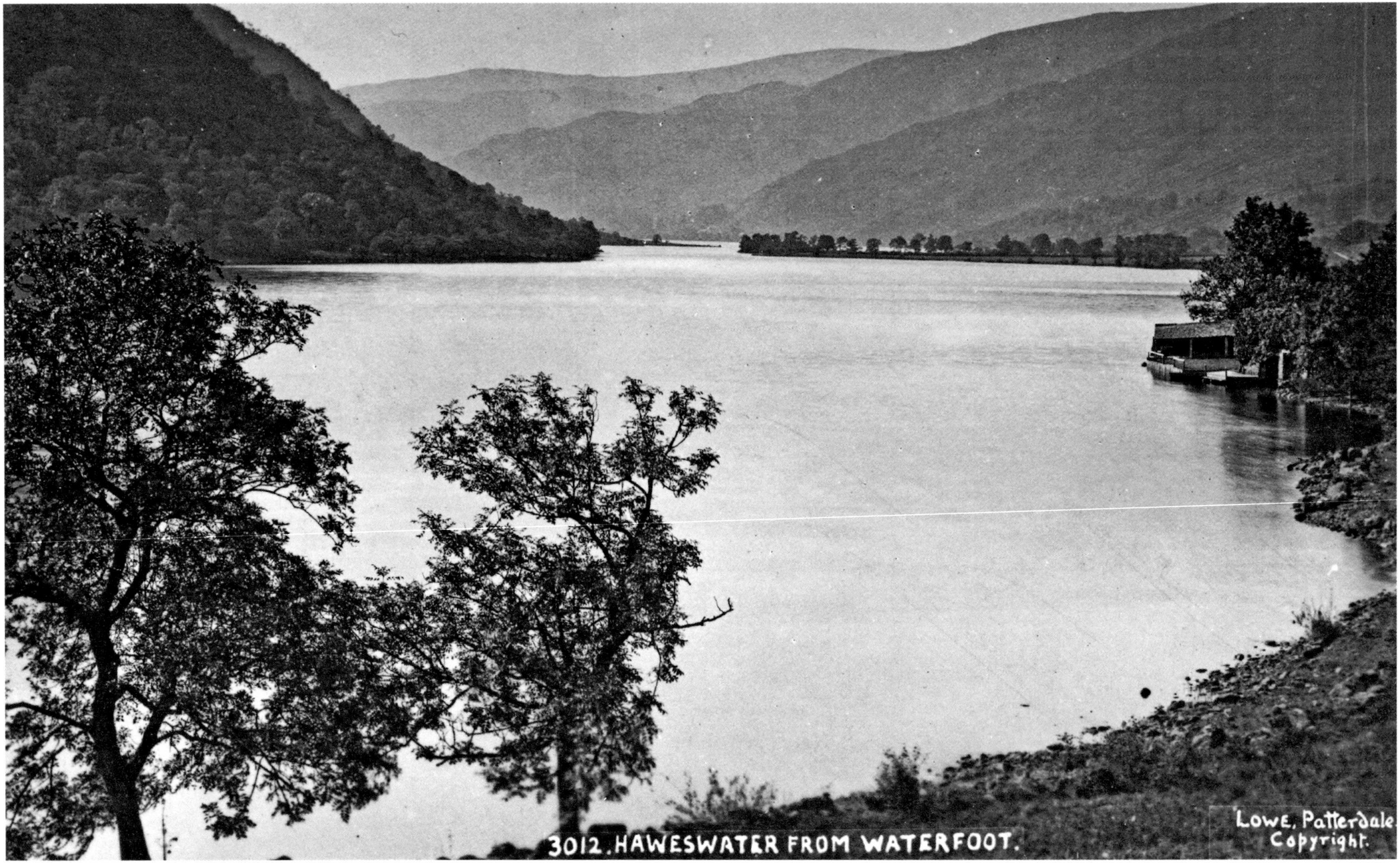

As the traveller entered the valley, he would have seen this view of the lake from the road. On the right is the boathouse, which replaced an earlier one near Walla Crag on the opposite side of the lake. Lord Lonsdale owned the fishing rights, and his boatmen usually lived at Measand. Two ancient residents of Haweswater are skelly and char, and a more recent addition are trout. In the distance, a line of trees marks the delta near Measand, where the Straits almost divided the lake. The natural lake was 2 ½ miles long.

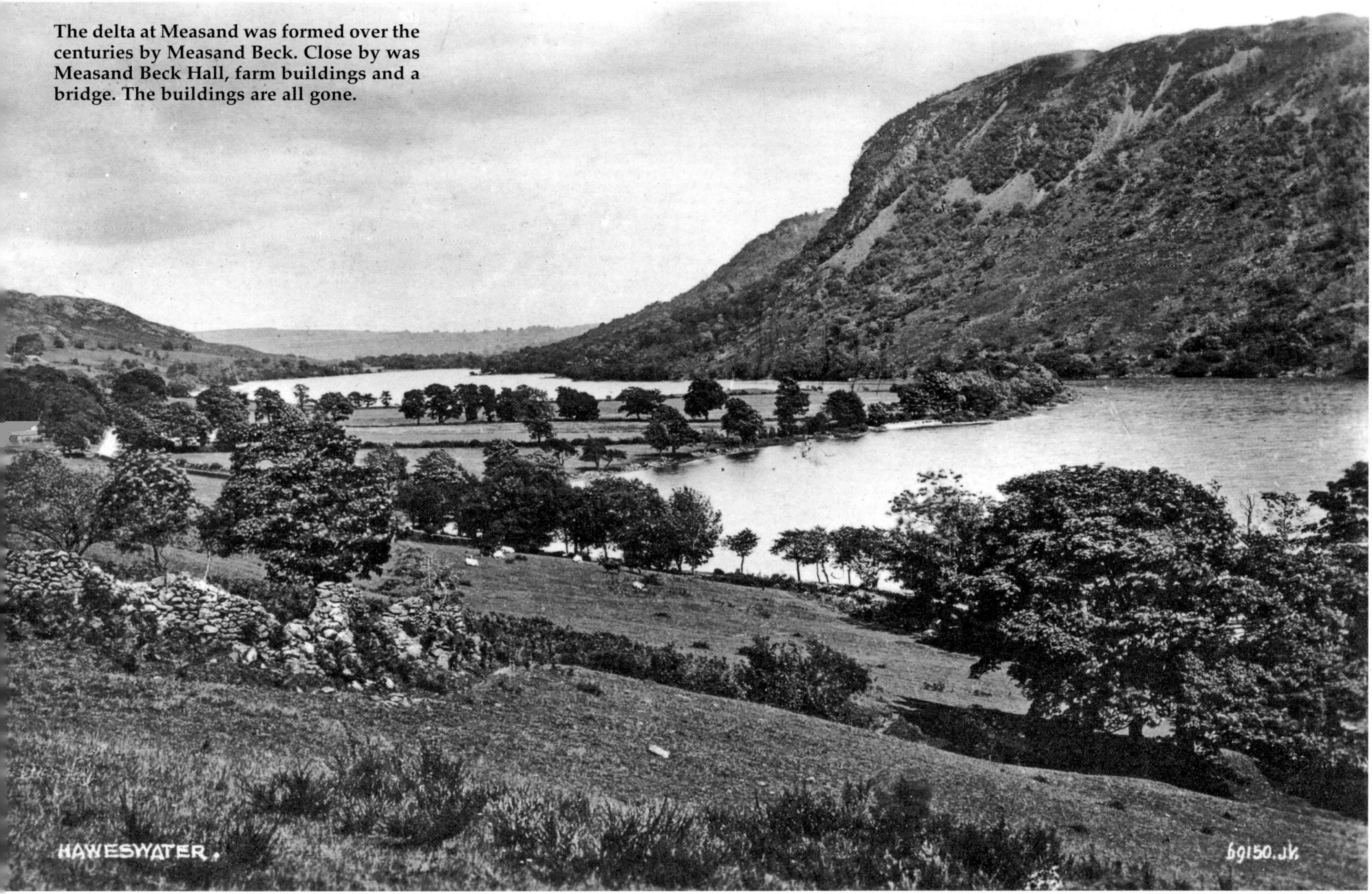

The delta at Measand was formed over the centuries by Measand Beck. Close by was Measand Beck Hall, farm buildings and a bridge. The buildings are all gone.

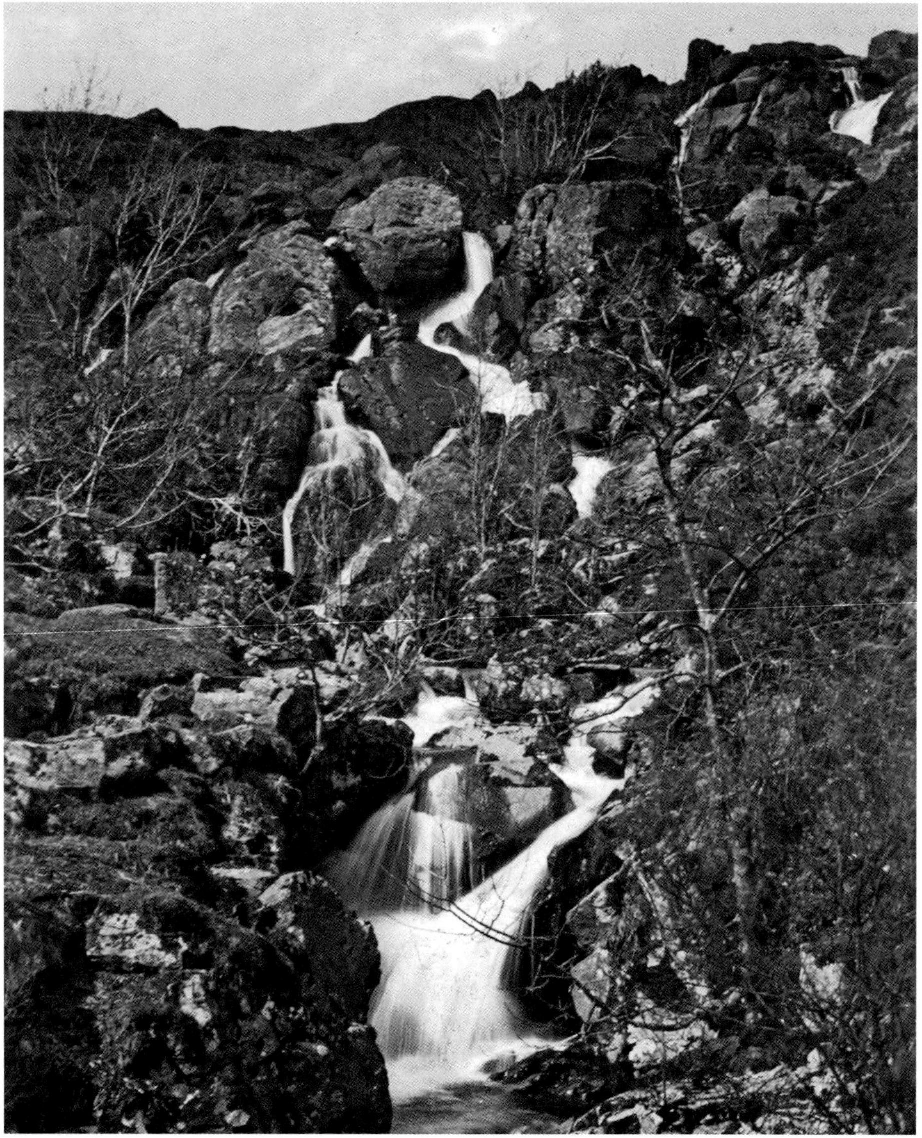

Measand Falls are still above the reservoir level, and they are spectacular after heavy rain, when viewed from the modern road on the other side of the lake. From the foot of the falls they form an impressive cascade over the rocks.

Opposite: The terrace at the top of the falls makes for a perfect viewpoint up the valley. Before the construction of the dam the view was a panorama of High Water with the tiny village at its head.

Below: A view into Riggindale from further up the valley.

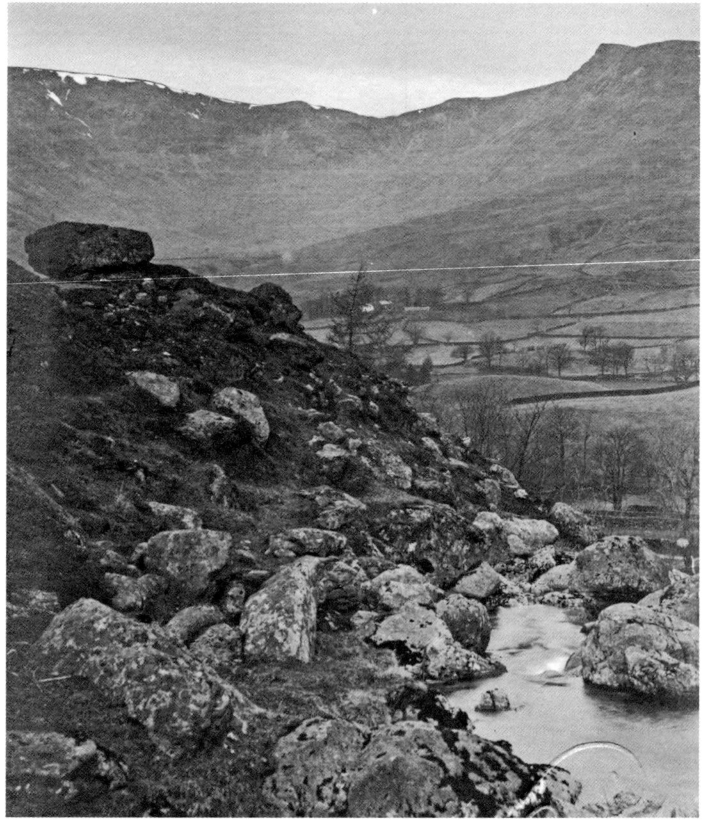

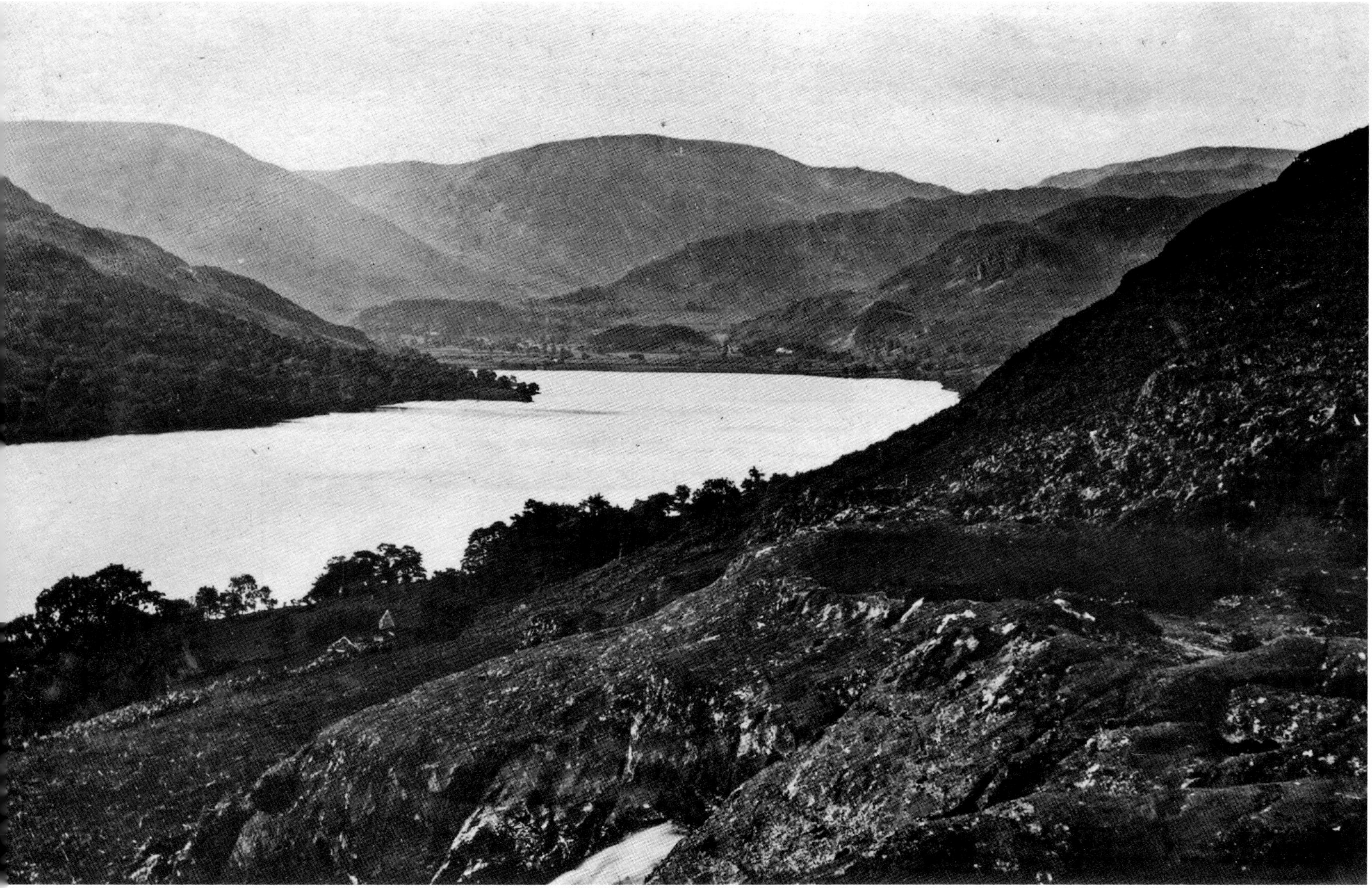

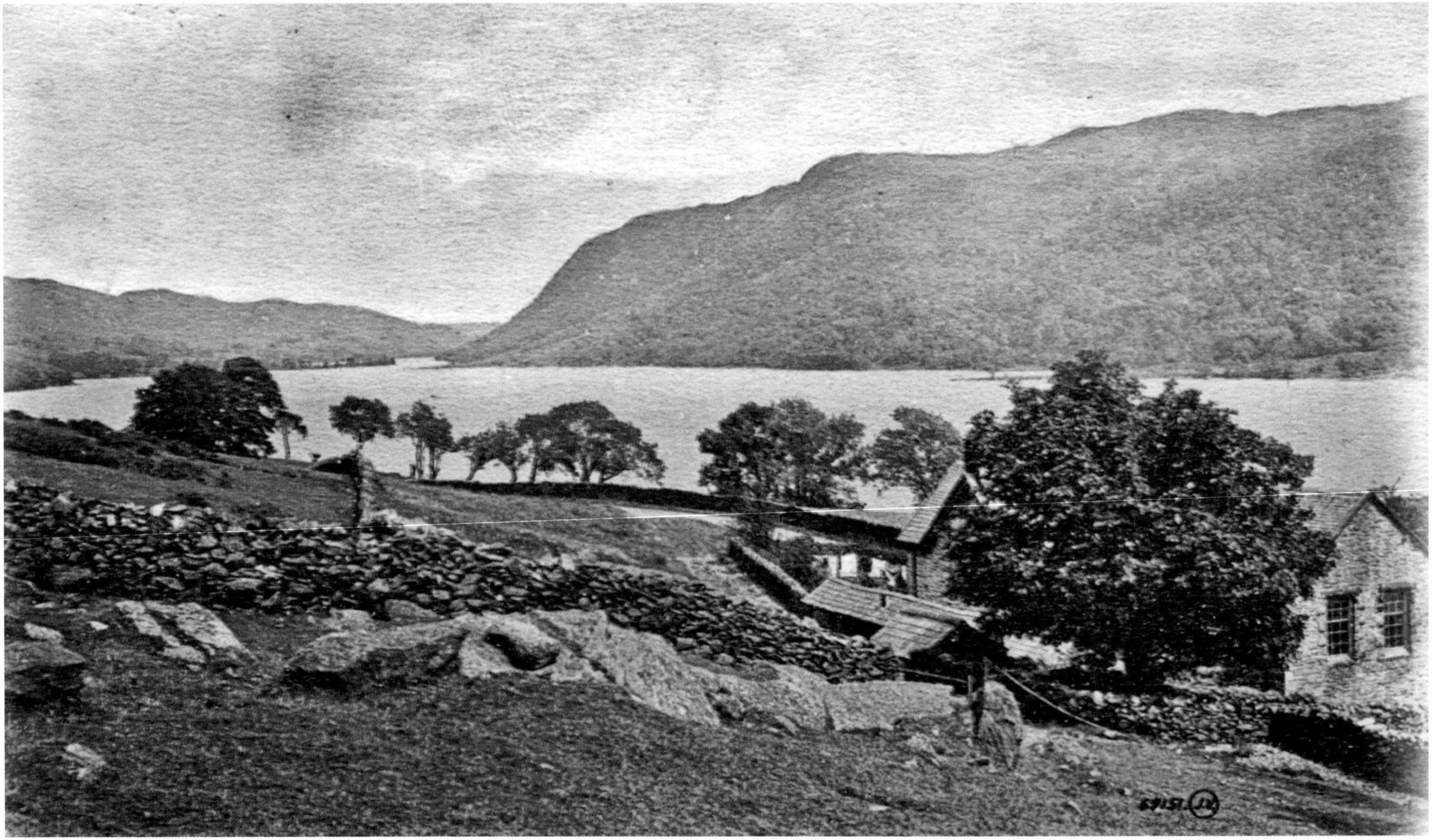

A view of Haweswater from above the school, which stood a little further along the road from Measand. It seems odd that such a tiny community could boast a school, but this building was founded by Richard Wright in 1711 at a time when many more people lived in the valley. Measand Grammar School had room for only a dozen or so pupils, but in the 19th century it gained a reputation as a theological college, and sent several scholars to Cambridge. The last school mistress was Miss Jane Foster, who was appointed in 1891 at the age of 23. She remained at the school until its closure in 1932. The school was threatened by the proposed flooding, but a wellwisher paid for the building to be dismantled and rebuilt at Walmgate Head near Burnbanks. It is the only building from the "old" Mardale to have survived.

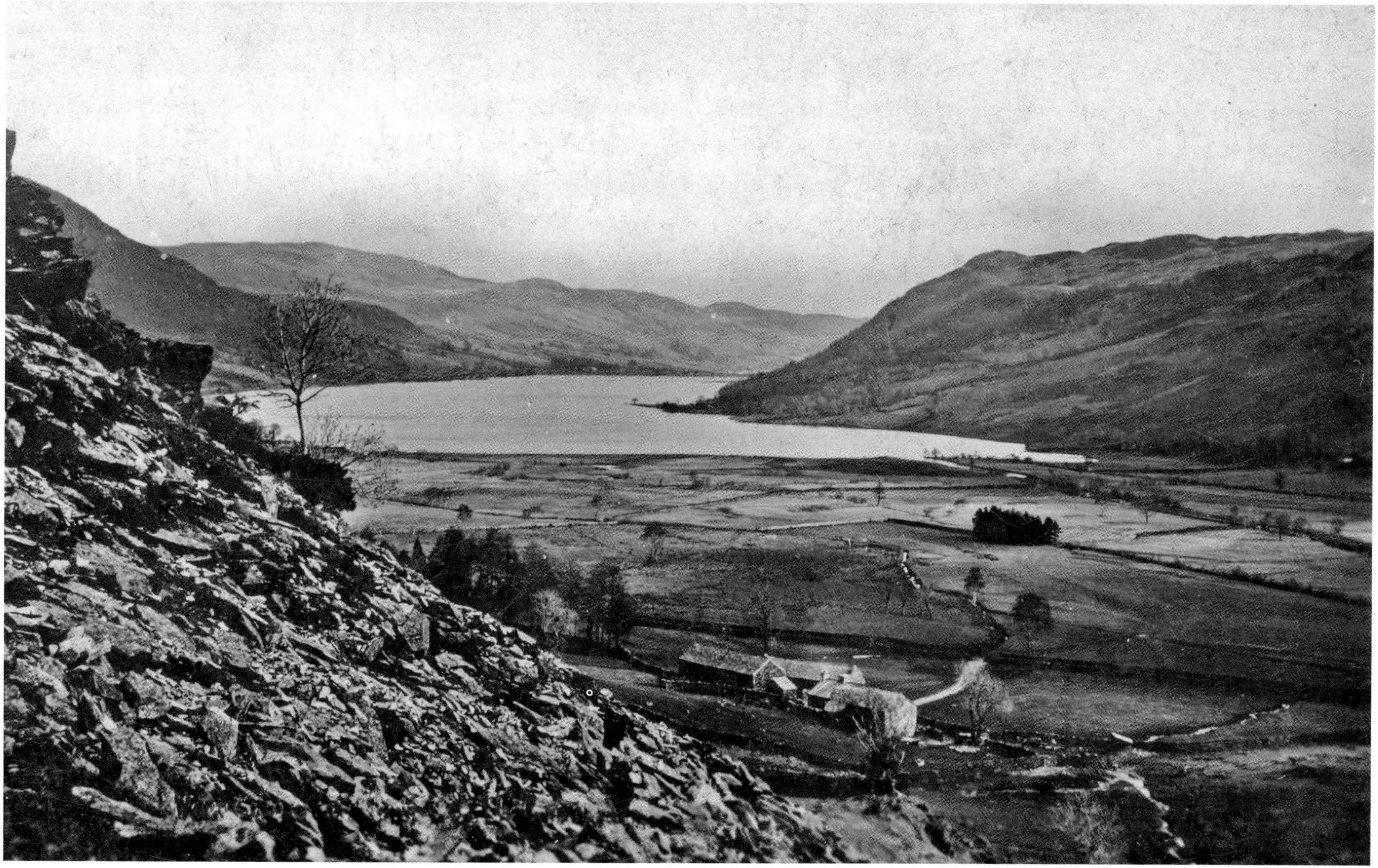

Mardale was probably first settled during the Bronze Age. These early peoples would have found plenty of wood for shelters, and fish, waterfowl and deer for food. In times of danger they would have moved to a fortified site on Castle Crag, high above the lake, which may still be seen. The view above is from this rocky promontory, with Flakehow Farm below in the valley.

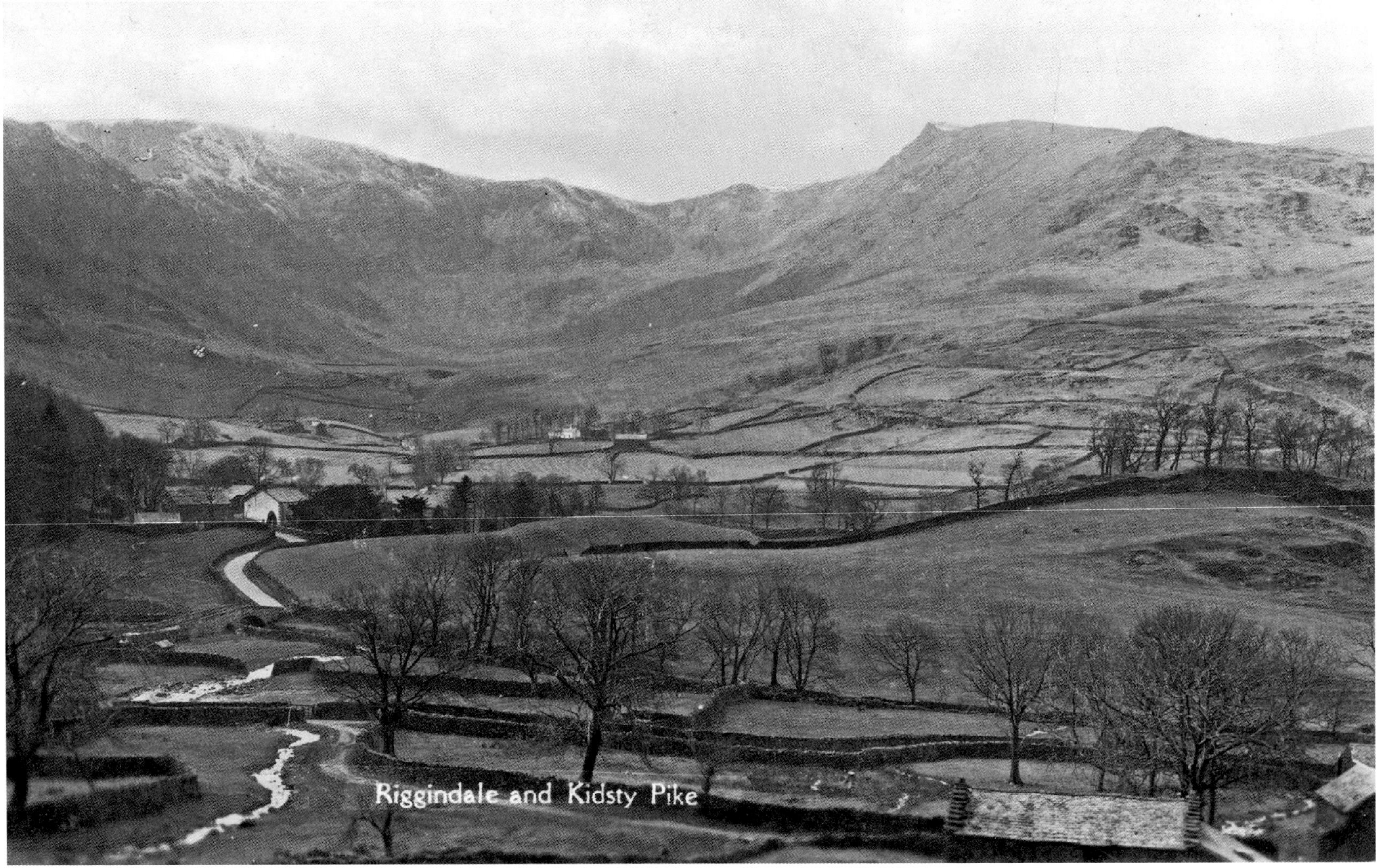

This view, taken above Grove Brae and Goosemire Farms, looks across the Mardale Valley into the smaller valley of Riggindale. Riggindale Farm may just be seen in the distance, with High Street and Kidsty Pike high above. Before the flooding, the farm was used largely as a holiday home, but the buildings were demolished, leaving just one outbuilding remaining. Of late, Riggindale has become well-known as the home of the only golden eagles in England.

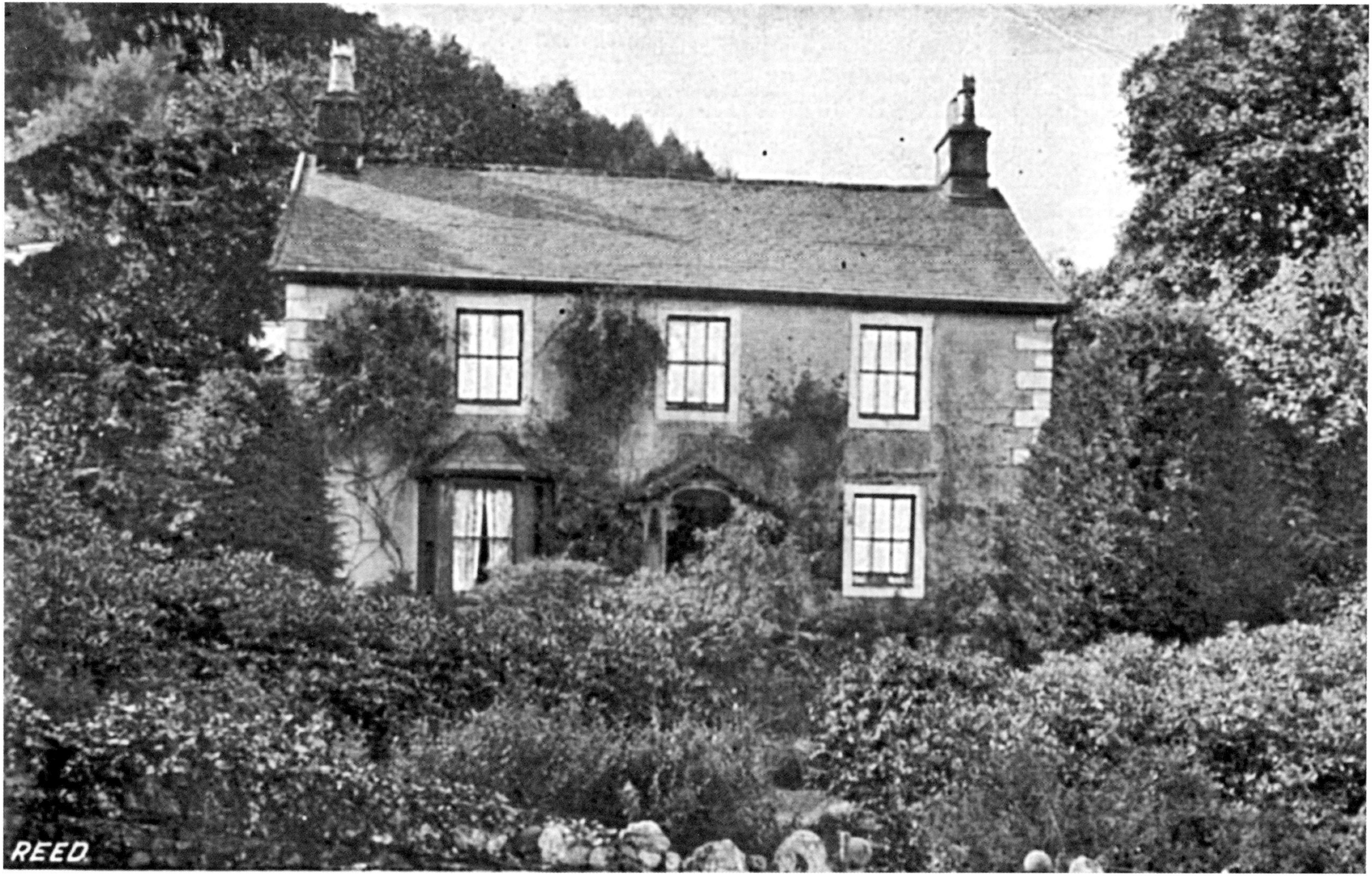

As the road neared Mardale Church, a small cluster of buildings were visible on the wooded side of the Rigg, one of which was this impressive farm, Chapel Hill which probably dated from the 17th century. The last to farm here were the Hudsons. In 1933, when the valley was abandoned, Chapel Hill and Flakehow Farm were used as youth hostels - one for men, the other for women. Soon afterwards both farms were blown up by the local Territorials.

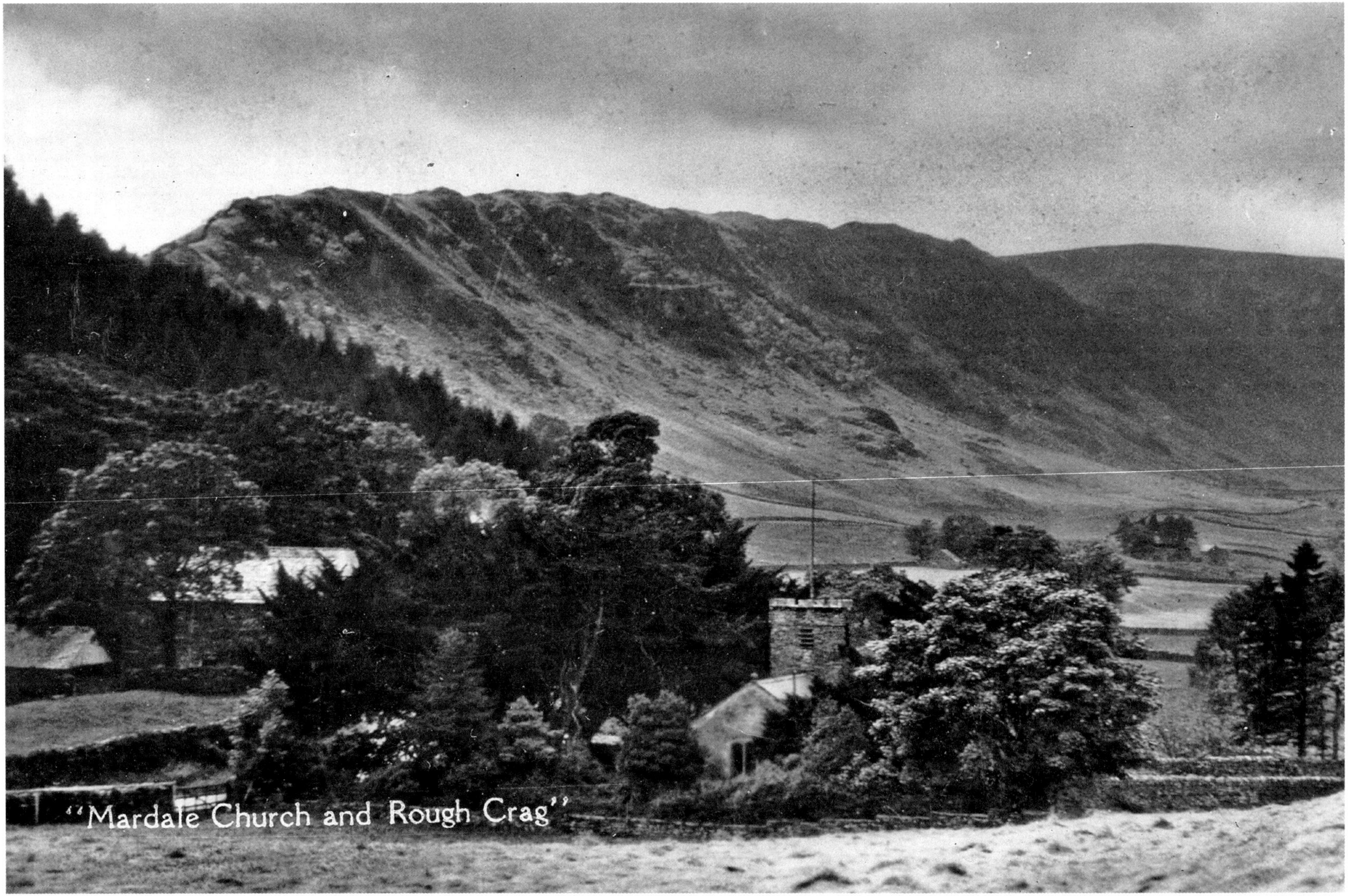

Chapel Hill Farm hidden among treees on the left and, in the centre, Mardale Church across the road. Rough Crag rises dramatically in the background.

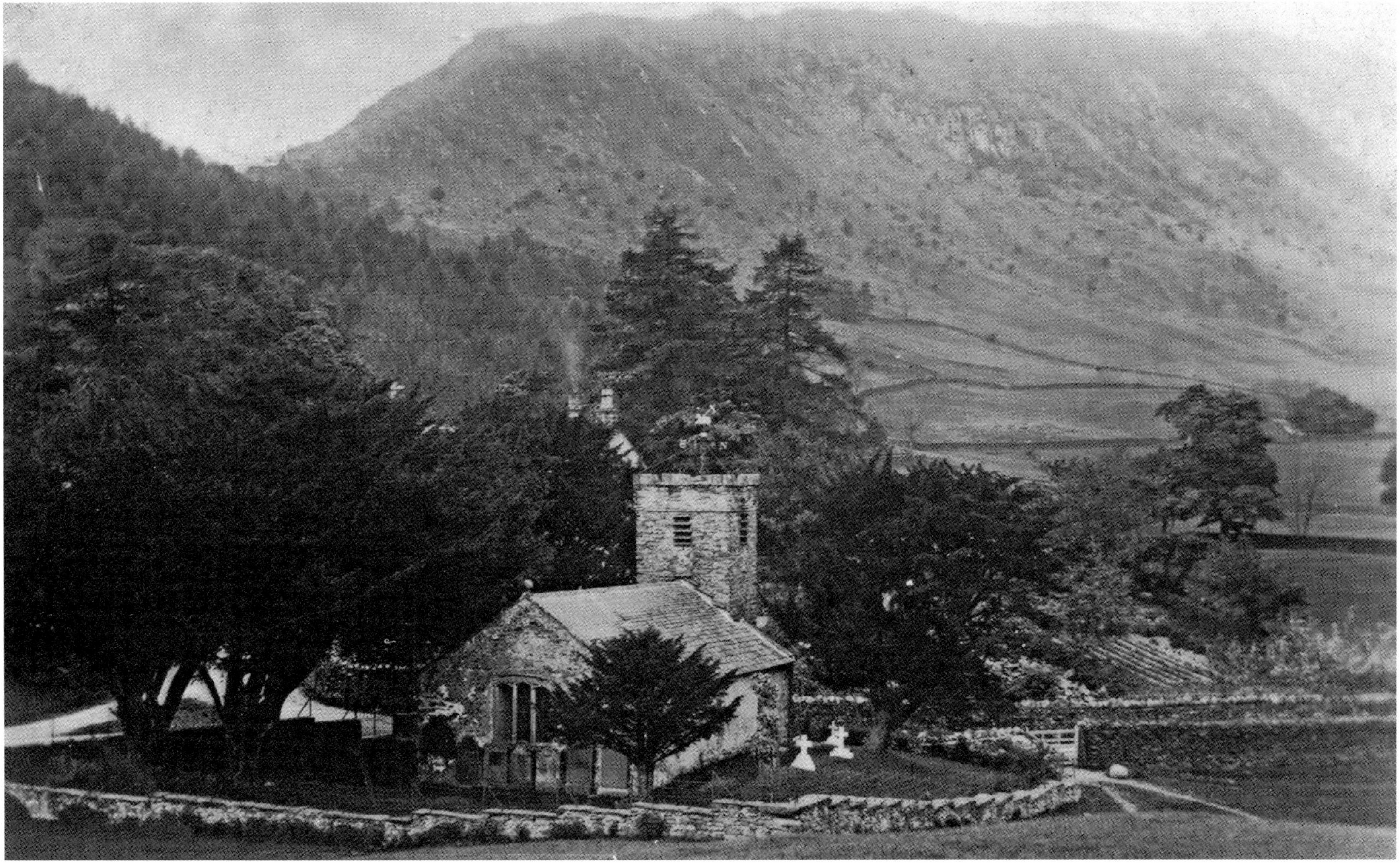

During the 14th century, monks from Shap Abbey built an oratory on Chapel Hill and planted six yew trees. Wood from these trees was needed for long bows for the Kendal archers. Towards the end of the 17th century, the tiny Mardale Church, dedicated to the Holy Trinity, was constructed. Its walls were three feet thick and it was broad and low, typical of other Lakeland churches such as Wasdalehead and Swindale. The church tower was only 29 1/2 feet high. A bell was installed in 1825.

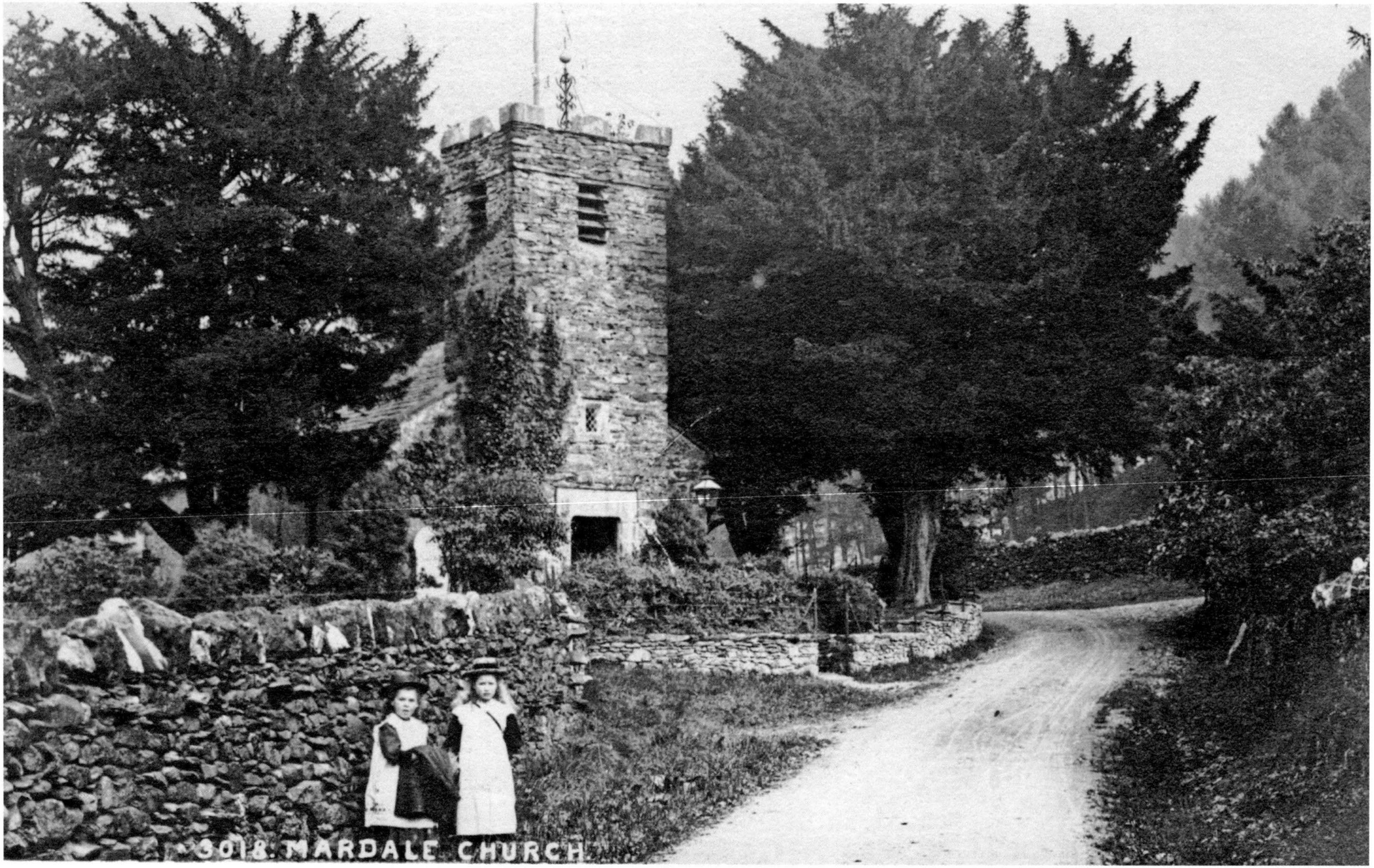

This delightful photo, taken by Lowe of Patterdale, shows two young girls posing by the walls adjoining Mardale Church. Perhaps they were local girls, as this photo was taken before the First World War and before Manchester's plans for the valley were public knowledge. Mardale's little church is truly dwarfed by the yew trees in this scene. In the drought of 1995, the stumps of the trees could still be seen.

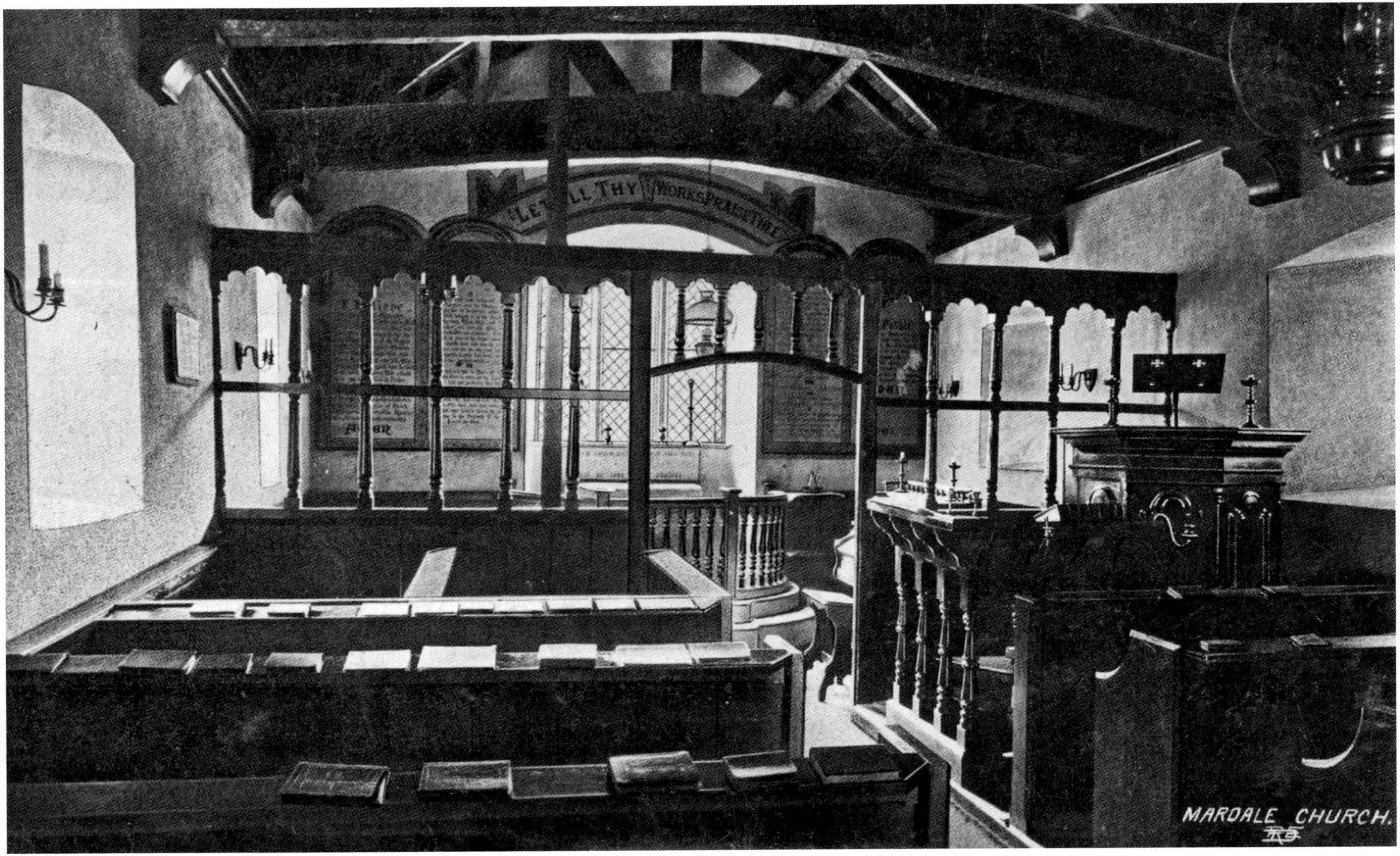

The interior of Holy Trinity Church. The family box pews provided seating for about 50 people, though when the final service took place in 1936 tickets for 70 people were issued. The church enjoyed its heyday in the 1890s, when oil and paraffin lamps illuminated the building, a new organ was purchased, and annual choir and Sunday school excursions were arranged. The Revd F.J.H. Barham, the last vicar of Mardale, even played gramophone records in the church!

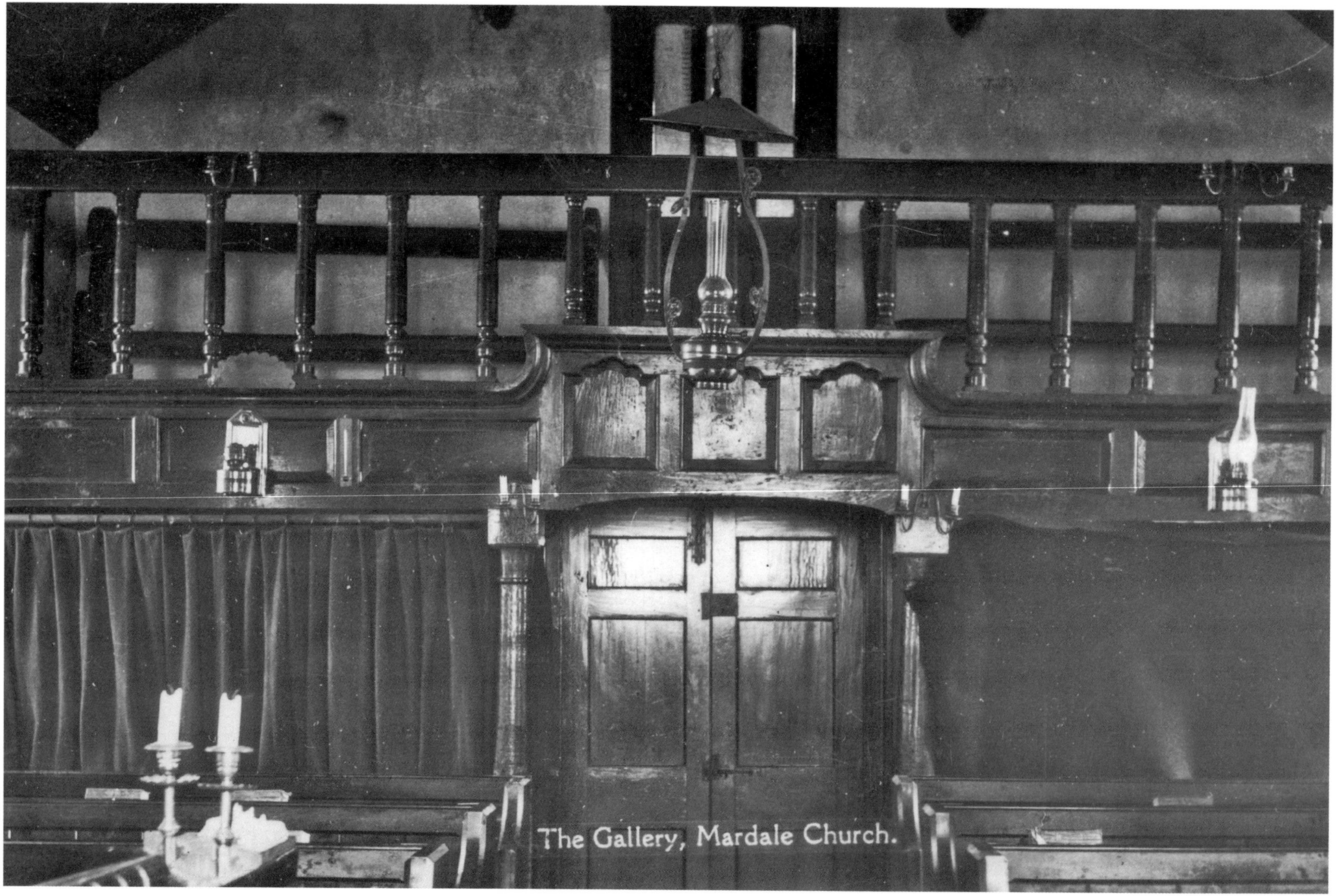

In 1737 an oak gallery, screen and communion rails were installed at the rear of the church.

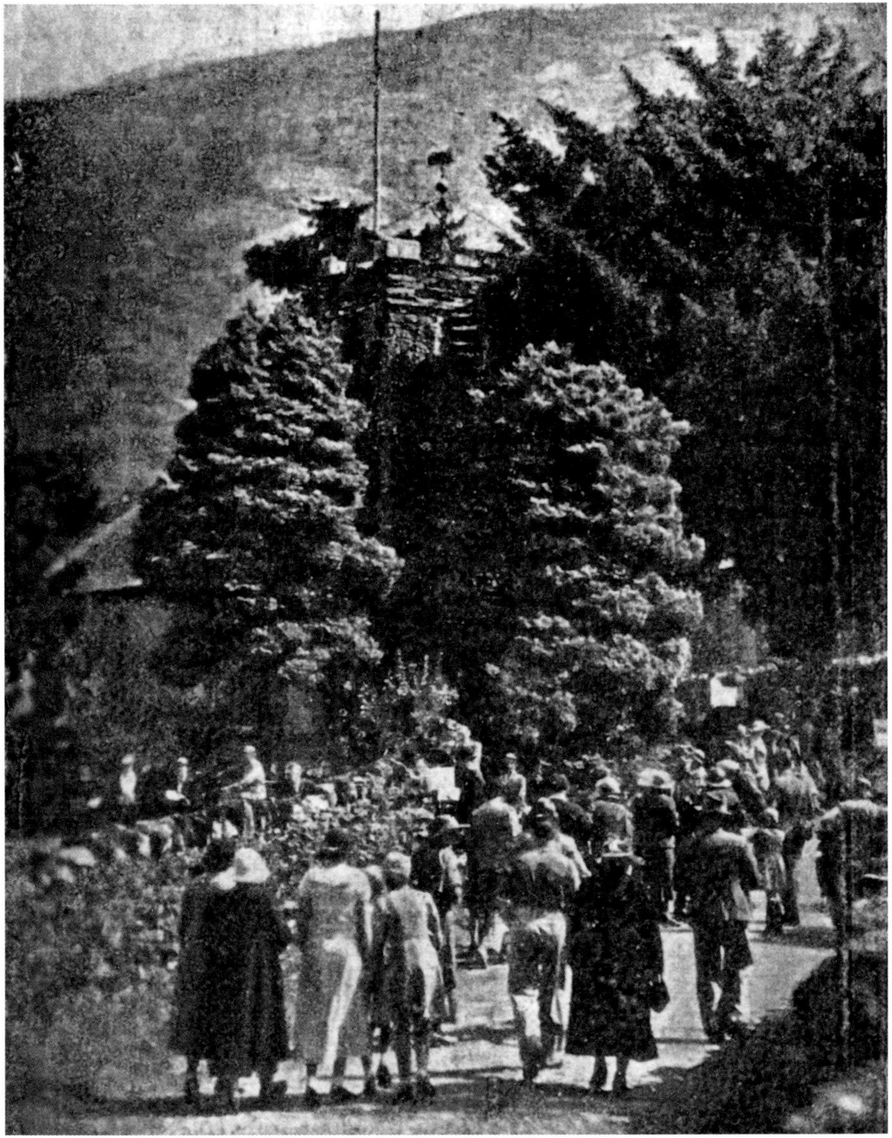

The final service took place at Holy Trinity Church on the 18th of August, 1935. The traffic from several thousand visitors choked the road that led to the church. The service was conducted jointly by the vicars of Bampton and Shap. The Bishop of Carlisle was asked to preach the sermon, but the Revd F.J.H. Barham was not invited to take part in the service. He spent the afternoon wandering among the thousands of people who had travelled to Mardale to witness this final act. Loudspeakers were fixed to the church tower, so that everybody could follow the service. The hymns included "I will lift up mine eyes unto the hills" and "O God our Help in Ages Past." The bishop did not weep for Mardale, but stressed that sacrifices were needed to help the large urban populations. He also opposed the removal of the church to another site as he preferred new churches in urban areas to a museum of old Mardalian ecclesiastical relics.

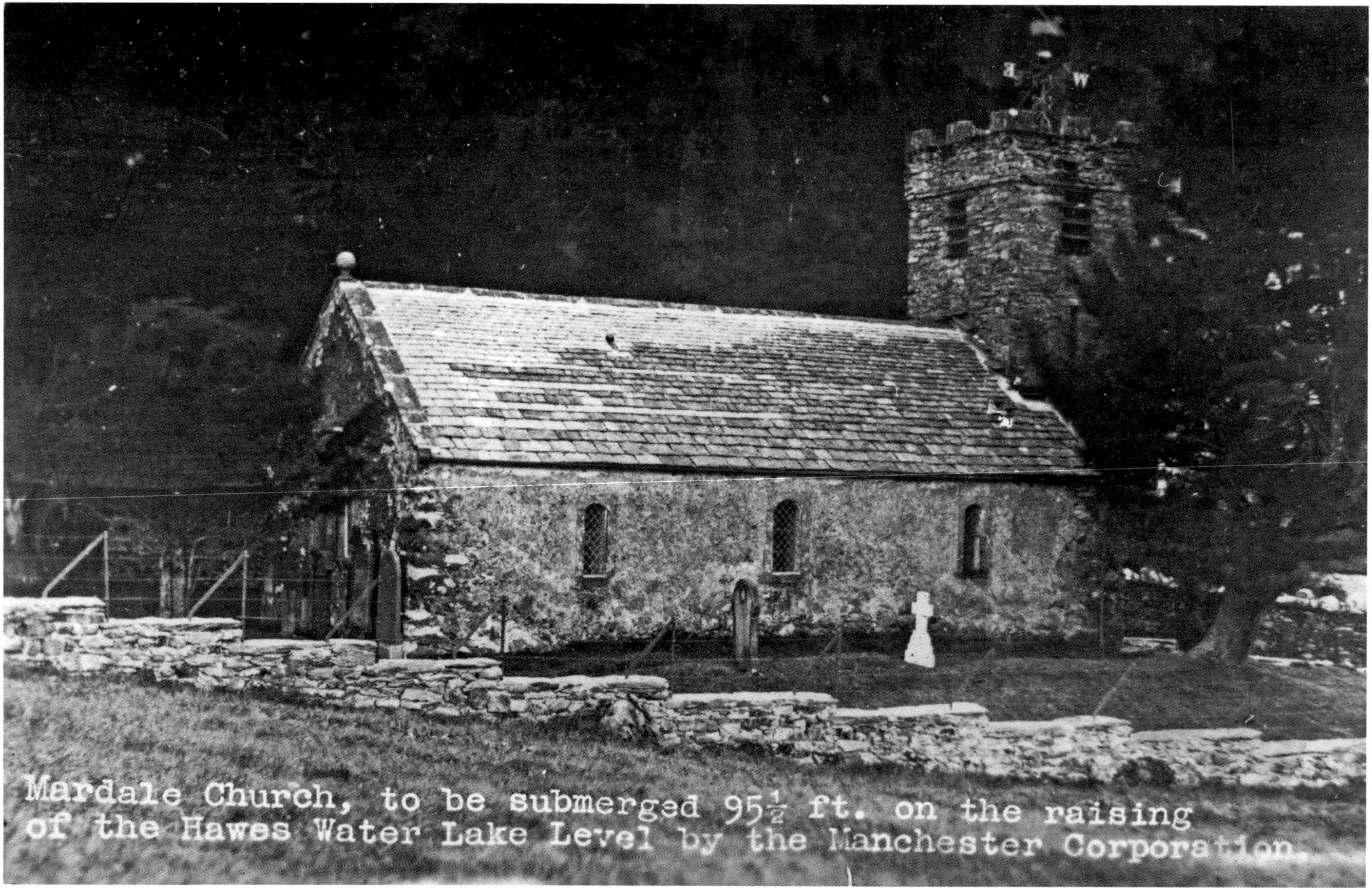

This is probably the last commercial postcard showing Mardale Church. This card was posted in 1937, some time after the church had been dismantled. In late 1935, the grim task of exhuming about a hundred bodies from the churchyard began.

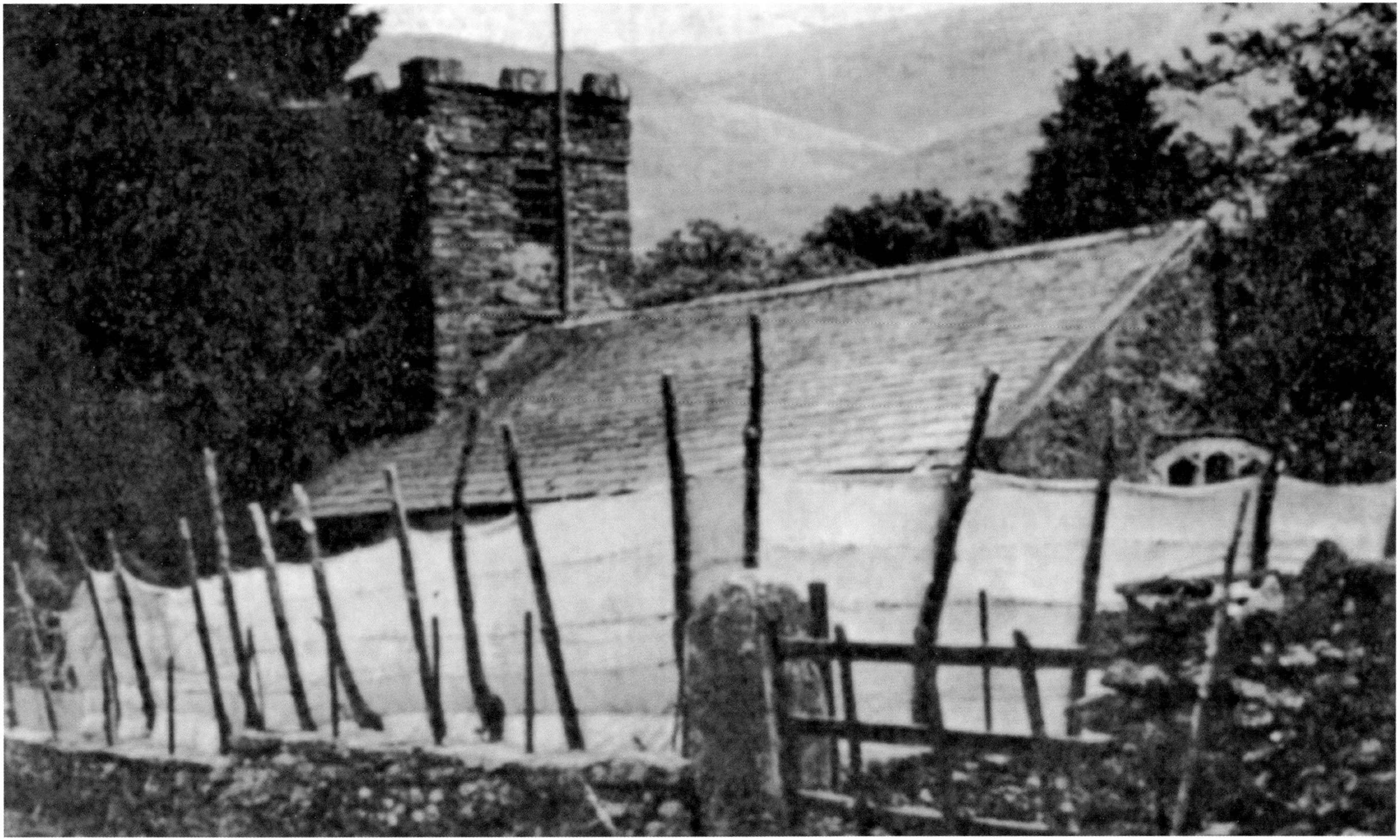

This photograph shows the screen that was erected around the church while the bodies were removed. Most of them were reinterred in a separate section of the cemetery at Shap and some of the headstones and plaques were arranged against a wall. A few bodies were buried elsewhere. Most of the furnishings of the church were transferred to the new Church of St. Barnabas at Carlisle, but the oak pulpit was acquired by Rosthwaite Church in Borrowdale and some of the black pews were made into seats in the new Haweswater Hotel. Last of all, the roof was removed and the church was dismantled stone by stone. Much of the stone and some of the windows were used in the construction of the new draw-off tower of the reservoir.

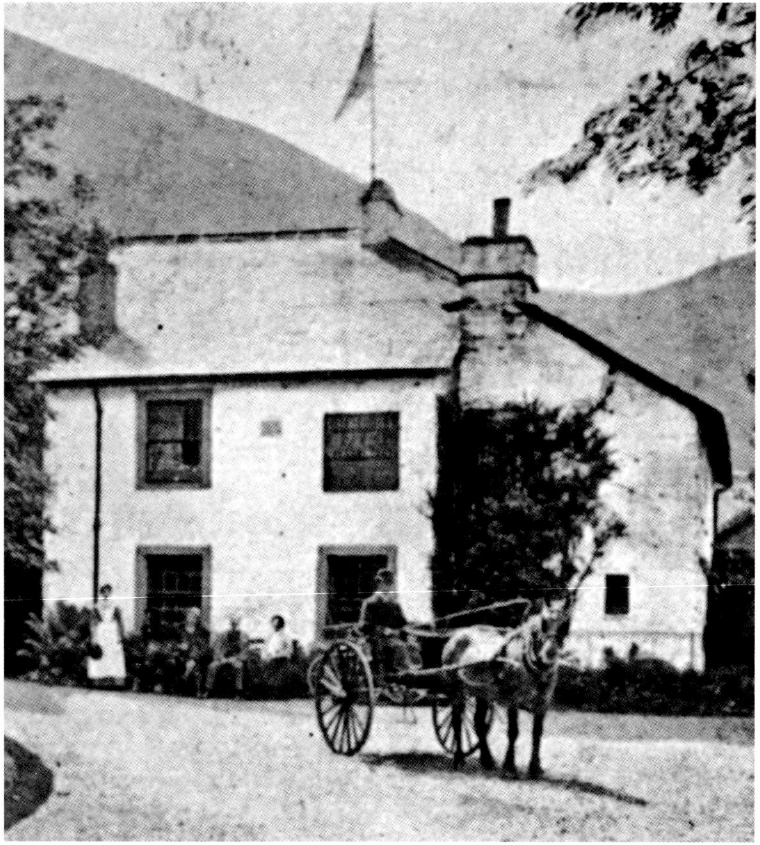

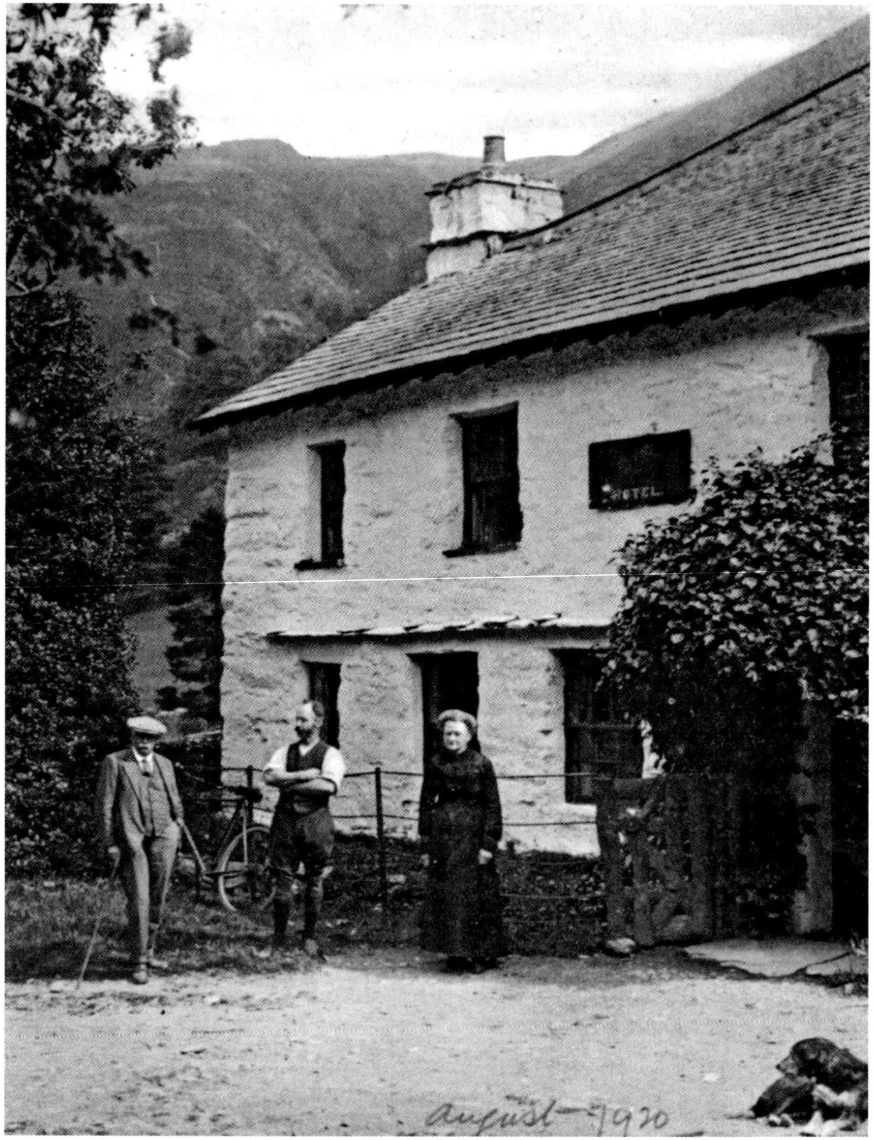

The Dun Bull Inn probably began life as a small Lakeland farm called "Greenhead" several hundred years ago, being sited at the junction of several of the hill tracks. Many of these early farms brewed ale for local shepherds and farm workers and for visiting walkers and anglers in the summer. There is evidence that other brew-houses once existed on the fells above the valley. Greenhead was extended in 1827 by its then tenant Thomas Lamley. By the 1851 census the building was usually called the Dun Bull Inn or Hotel. These photographs show the original farmhouse and Lakeland Inn. The picture on the right taken in 1920 shows the Daffurns, the hosts at the Dun Bull.

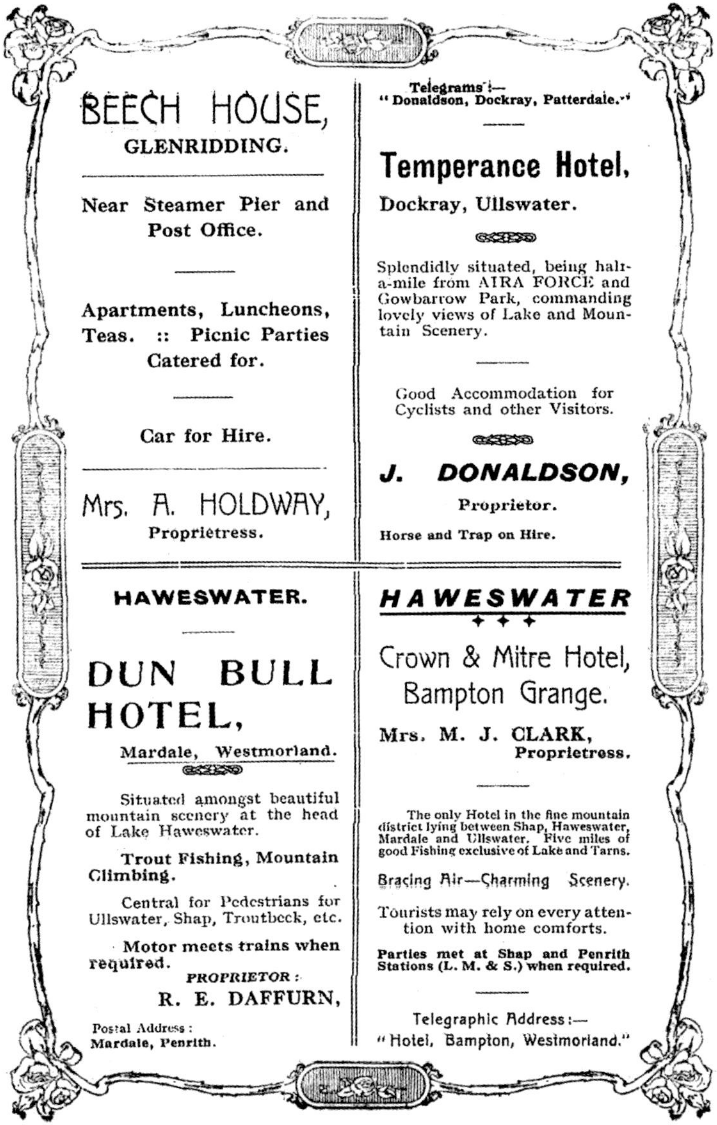

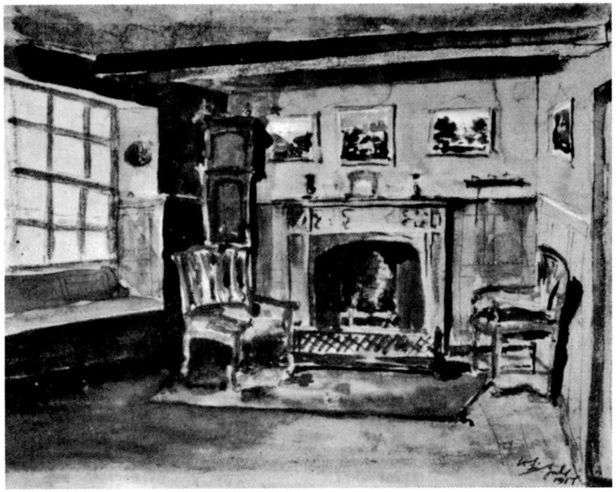

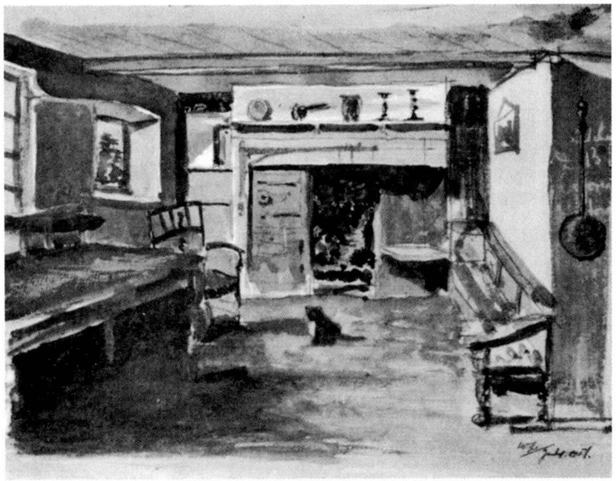

Bob Daffurn was the last landlord of the Dun Bull Hotel but was not a local man, having travelled from Wiltshire to become a gardener at Lowther Castle, married a local woman and stayed in the area. He took over the tenancy of the Dun Bull in 1906 and his time at the hotel saw the growing threat and final takeover of the valley by Manchester Corporation. The Dun Bull and the Crown and Mitre at Bampton both advertised in Lakeland guidebooks to attract tourists. As this Edwardian advert shows, both hotels offered transport to and from the nearby railway stations. Bob Daffurn initially used a stylish horse-drawn carriage (perhaps the one pictured on the front cover), but later preferred motorised transport. The water-colour sketches show the smoke room and kitchen of the Dun Bull in latter days. Bob Daffurn finally left in 1933 and took over the running of the Greyhound Inn at Shap, leaving his daughter, Mrs Lucy Bell to attend to the Dun Bull until it closed in 1935.

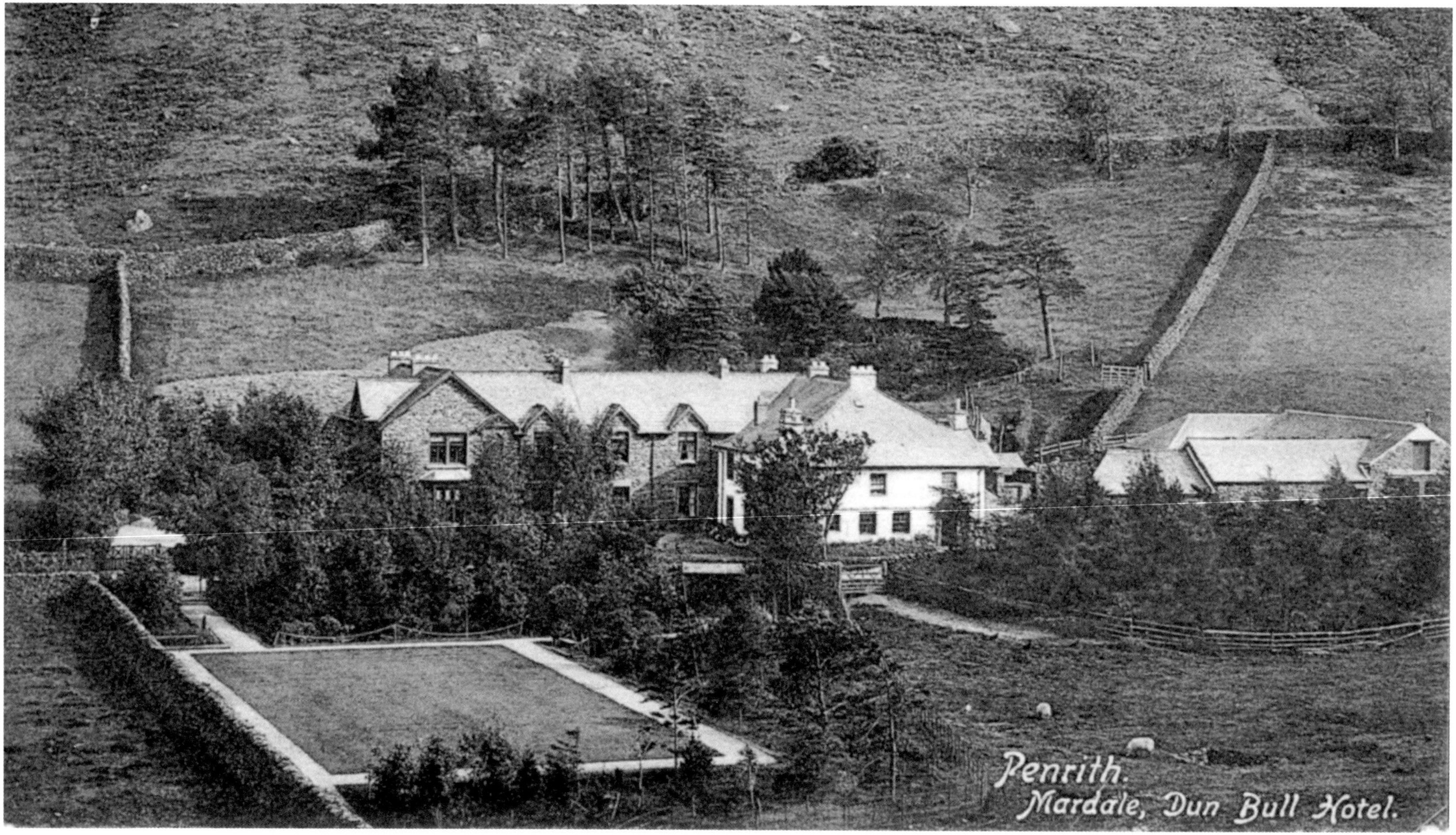

In the early 13th century, it is said that a certain Hugh Holme became involved in a conspiracy against King John, fled northwards towards Scotland, found refuge in Mardale, and stayed. His descendants became known as the "Kings of Mardale". Members of the family lived in various farms over the centuries and built Bowderthwaite on the southern flanks of Riggindale. This building was later used as an outbuilding by Chapel Hill Farm. In 1857 the Revd Thomas Holme built the Vicarage under Castle Crag, but after his death his widow had a new house constructed behind the Dun Bull Hotel. It was named Greenhead after the original farm, but was more generally known as "The Mansion". This card shows the location and size of The Mansion, and its tennis court. The postcard was posted in 1905 and the message reads: "On tramp for a day or two. This is the first place we put up at. Quite off the beaten track, about 15 miles from anywhere."

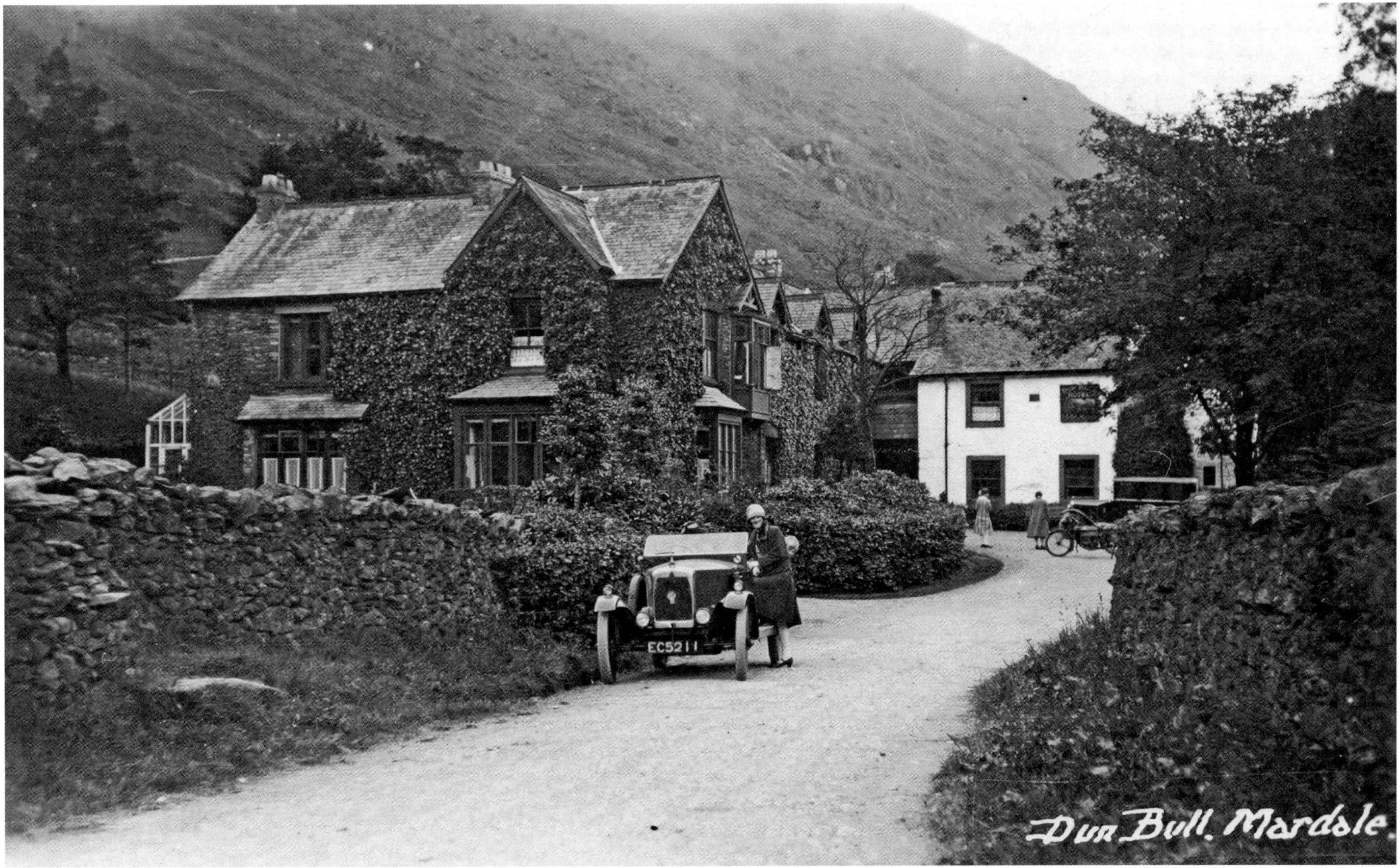

This photo, taken shortly before the closure of the Dun Bull, shows another view of Greenhead, the mansion which had been built by 1888. This building was unique in the valley, as it was constructed of dark-green limestone and left unrendered; all of the other Mardale houses and farms were limewashed. Mrs. Mary E. Holme, the widow of a former vicar, lived here with a companion and her staff for several years until ill-health forced her to move to Patterdale. After her death "The Mansion" was absorbed into the Dun Bull Hotel, which by then was catering for an increasing number of tourists.

The last "King", Hugh Parker Holme (the last in the male line of the Holme family), died in 1885. Sixty-four guests came to his funeral dinner in January 1886, and this is the bill - £9 2s 9d.

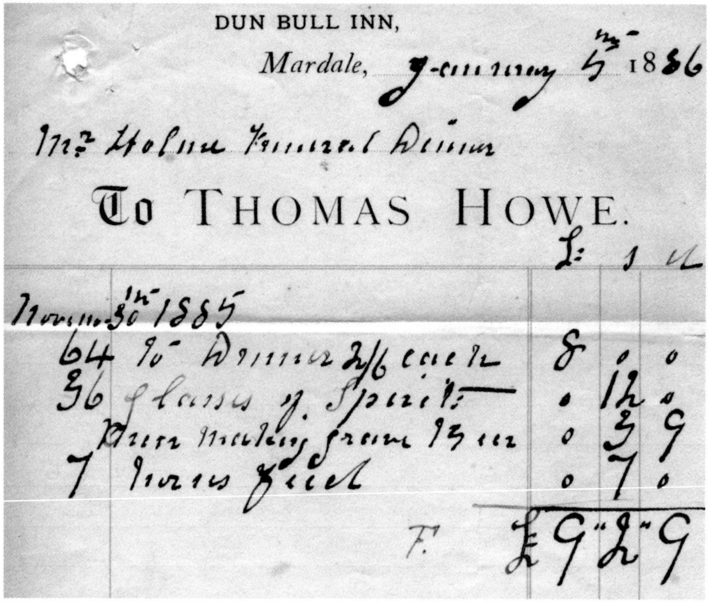

DUN BULL INN,

Mardale, January 5th 1886

Mrs Holme Funeral Dinner

To THOMAS HOWE.

	£	s	d
Novr 30th 1885			
64 to Dinner 2/6 each	8	0	0
36 Glasses of Spirits	0	12	0
Beer making from 13 [illegible]	0	3	9
7 Horses Feed	0	7	0
F.	£9	2	9

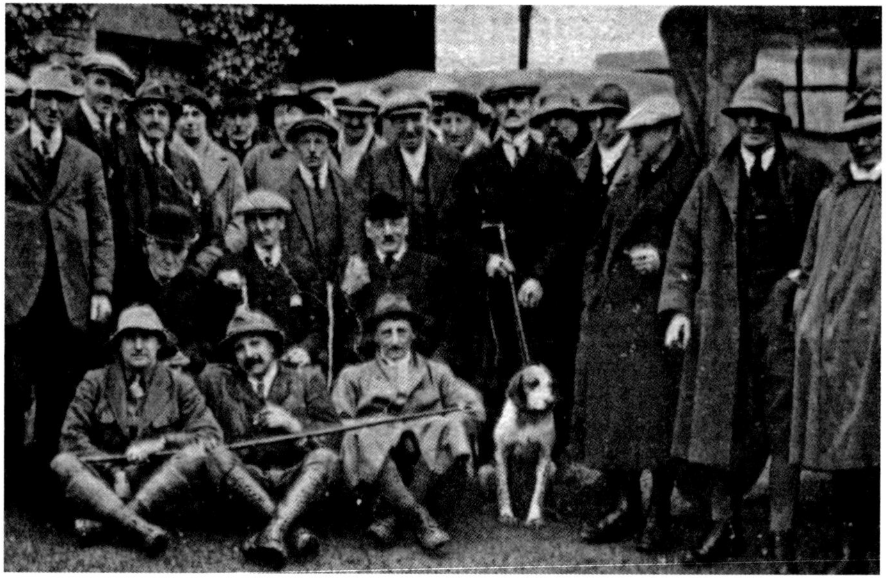

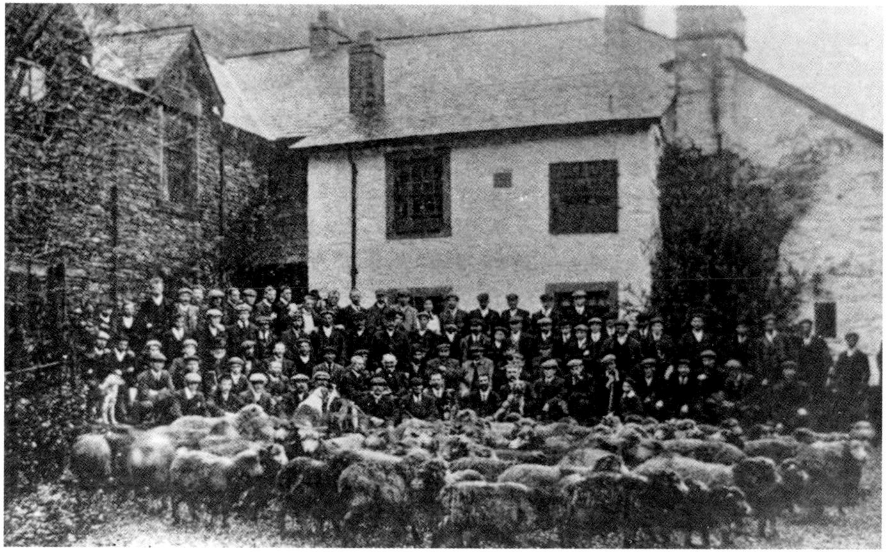

For almost a century there was an annual Shepherds' Meet at the Dun Bull Hotel in the third week in November. Stray sheep were brought in from surrounding fells and returned to their owners. Every farm had a distinctive mark; sheep were identified according to their ear or wool markings. In the old days, the Meet took place on the top of High Street. The formalities were accompanied by horse-racing, Cumberland and Westmorland wrestling, and other sports. In latter days the sport consisted of hunting, hound trails, sheep-dog trials and the like. Afterwards the men would repair to the Dun Bull for a feast, a smoking concert and a drink or two. Joe Bowman, the Master of the Ullswater Hunt, was a popular figure in these latter days; he was the best-known local huntsman after John Peel. Several hundred men attended the Meet in the 1920s and the beer had to be distributed in buckets! The last Meet took place there in 1935. One can only imagine the atmosphere at that very nostalgic event. Since then, the Mardale Meet has taken place every November at Bampton.

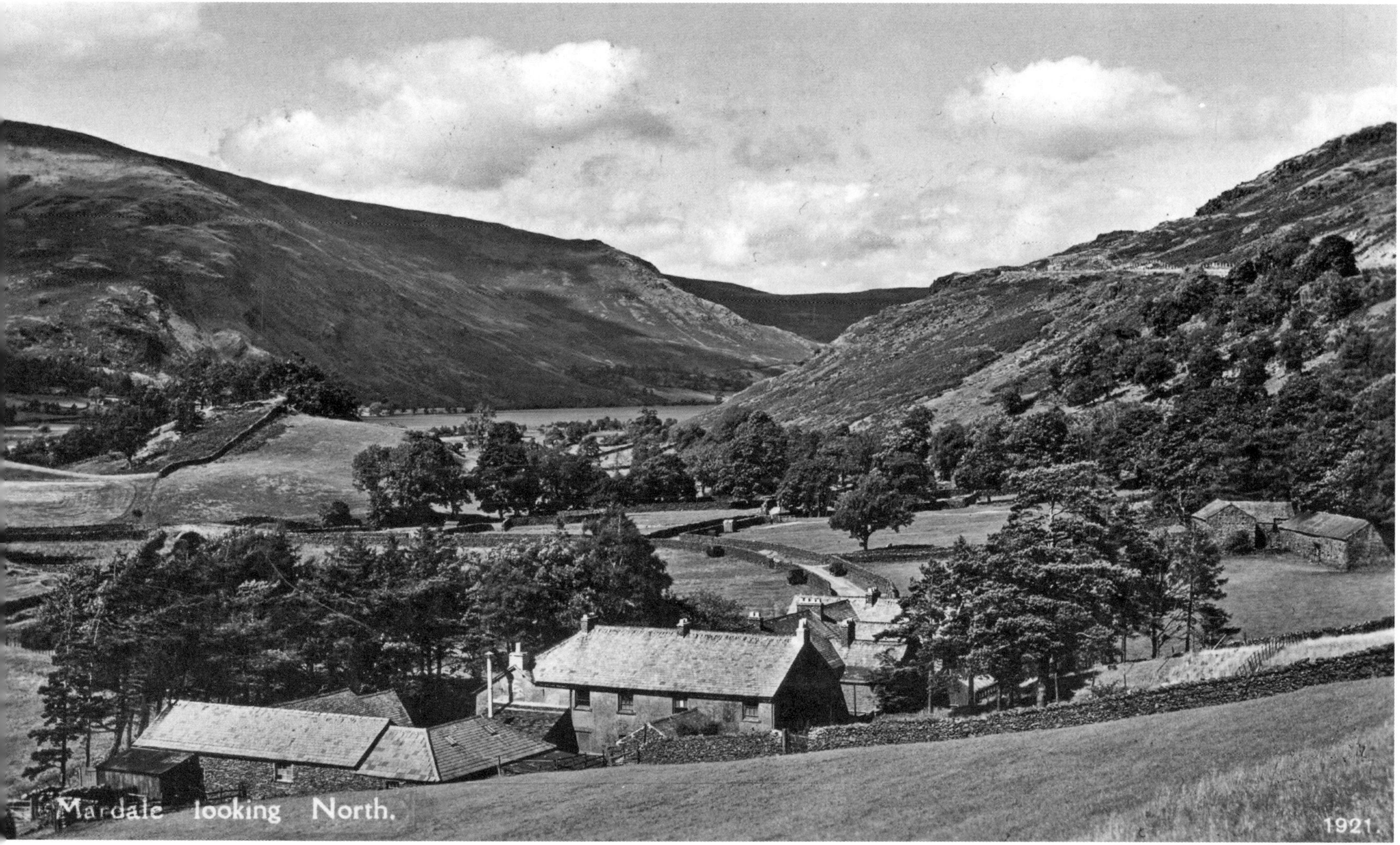

This view dates to the last years of the Dun Bull, seen in the foreground. The new road to the head of the valley had been constructed by 1931. It may seen near the top right of the photo, many feet above the buildings that would soon be underwater. This card was posted in 1935, shortly before the Dun Bull Hotel closed its doors for the last time.

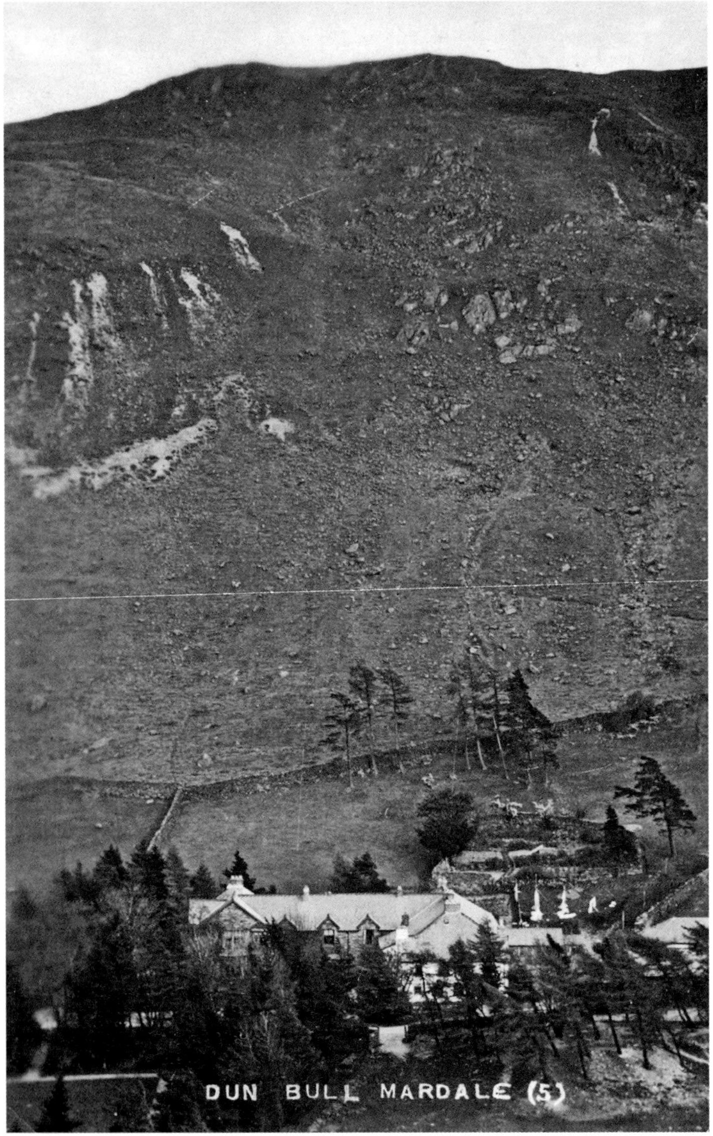

The postcard on the left shows the dramatic location of the Dun Bull Hotel. The card was posted in 1915 and part of the message on the back reads: "You will see the house, well that is as far as you can get and I got this pc [postcard] there. It is such a big hill at the back. The Lake Mardale is so pretty and the rocks and hills remind me a little bit of Ireland."

The photograph below shows a roofless Dun Bull, waiting for the final destruction.

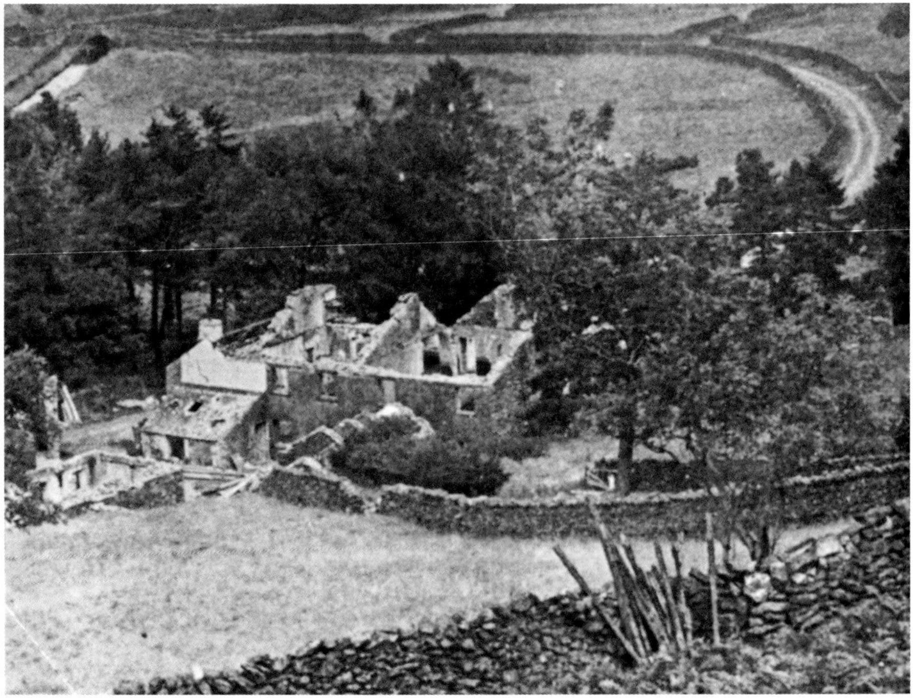

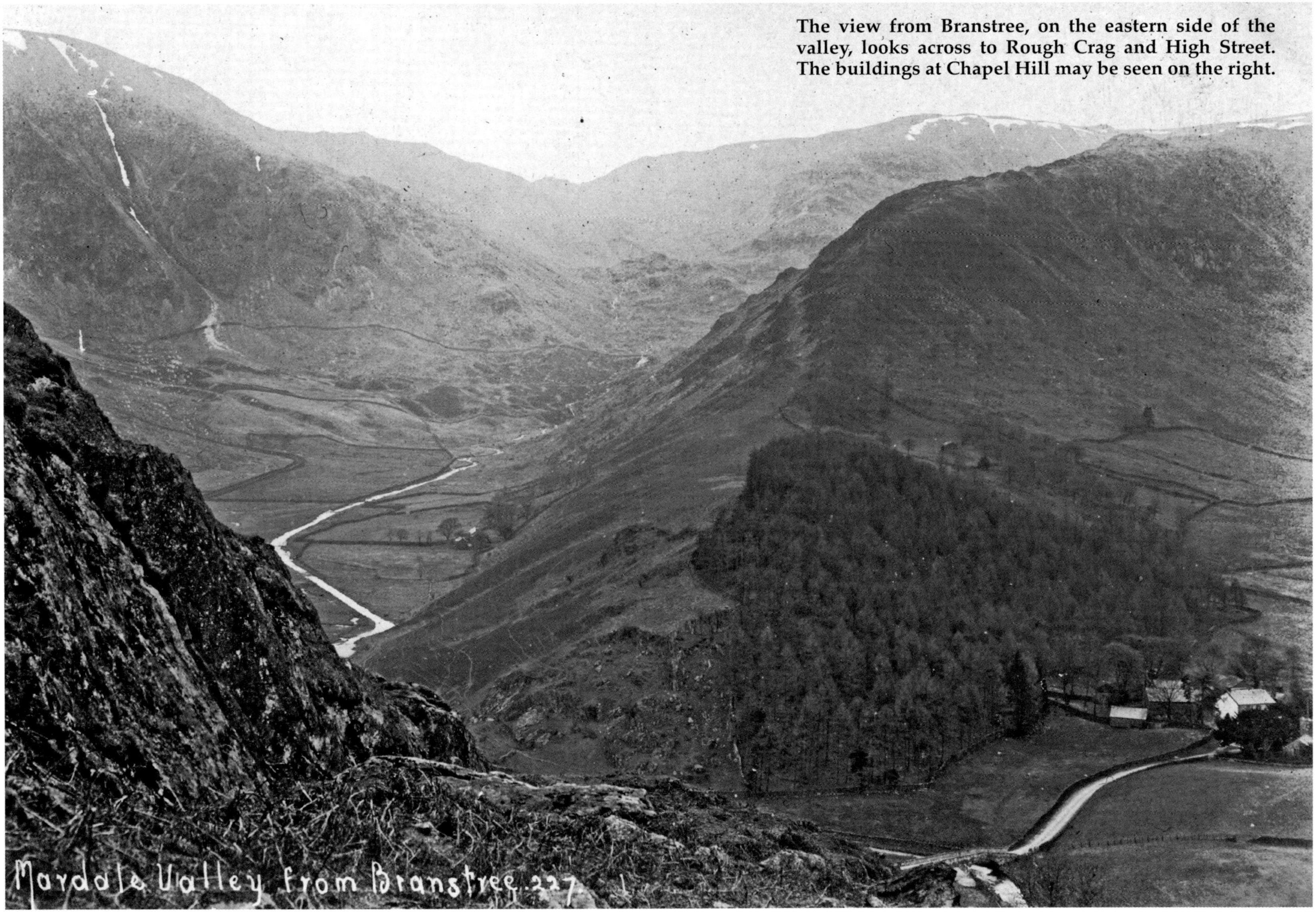

The view from Branstree, on the eastern side of the valley, looks across to Rough Crag and High Street. The buildings at Chapel Hill may be seen on the right.

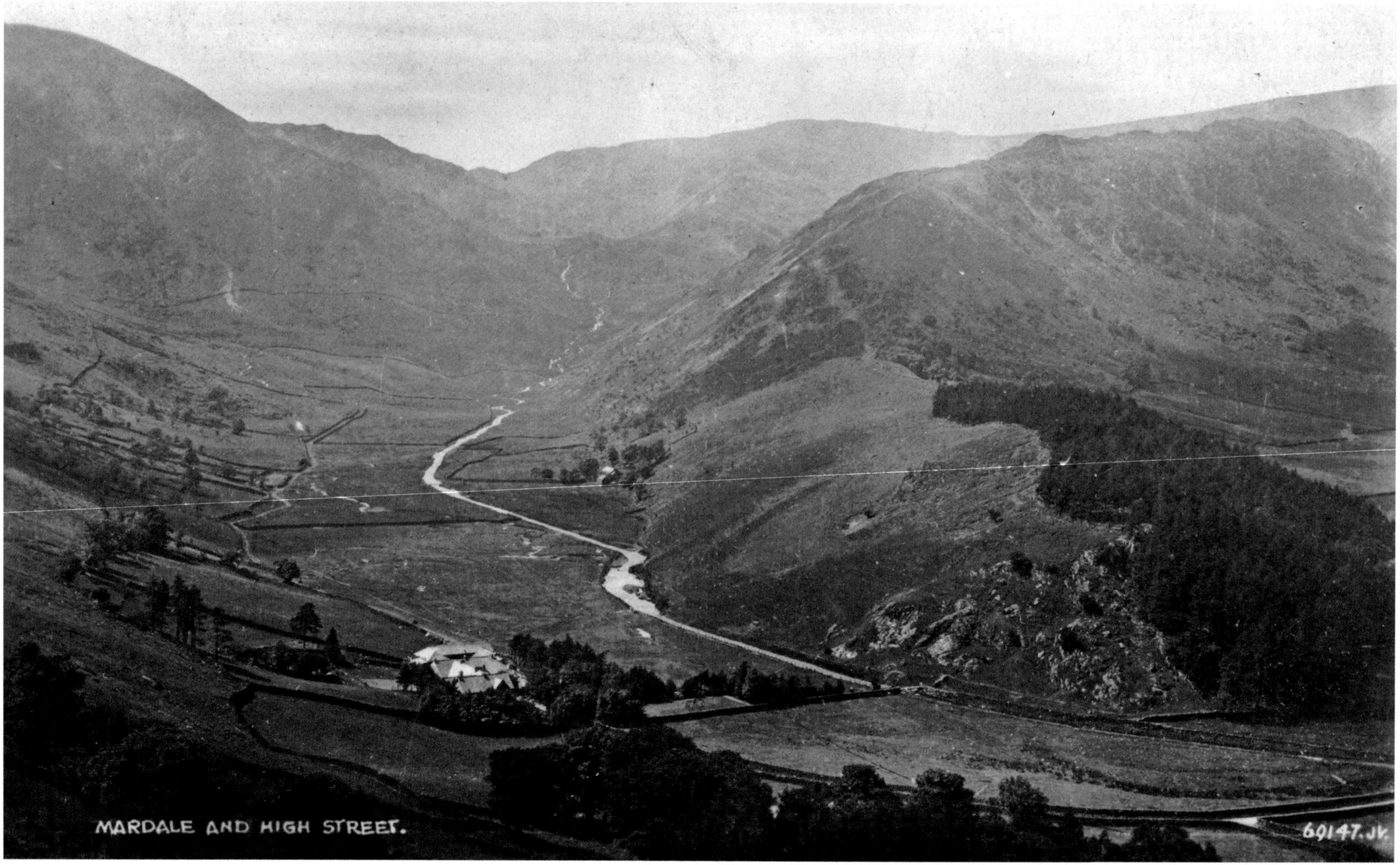

One of the major passes, Gatesgarth, ran by Harter Fell (the mountain on the left) over to Longsleddale Valley. This was a major packhorse route, linking Kendal with the north. Harter Fell was about 1800 feet above the Dun Bull (in the centre with the tennis court), and about a mile away as the crow flies. The other pass above the head of the valley is Nan Bield Pass, reached by climbing to the right. It gave access to the Kentmere Valley and to Kendal, and again was an important packhorse route. The pass also leads to High Street, the old Roman road linking Ambleside with forts near Penrith.

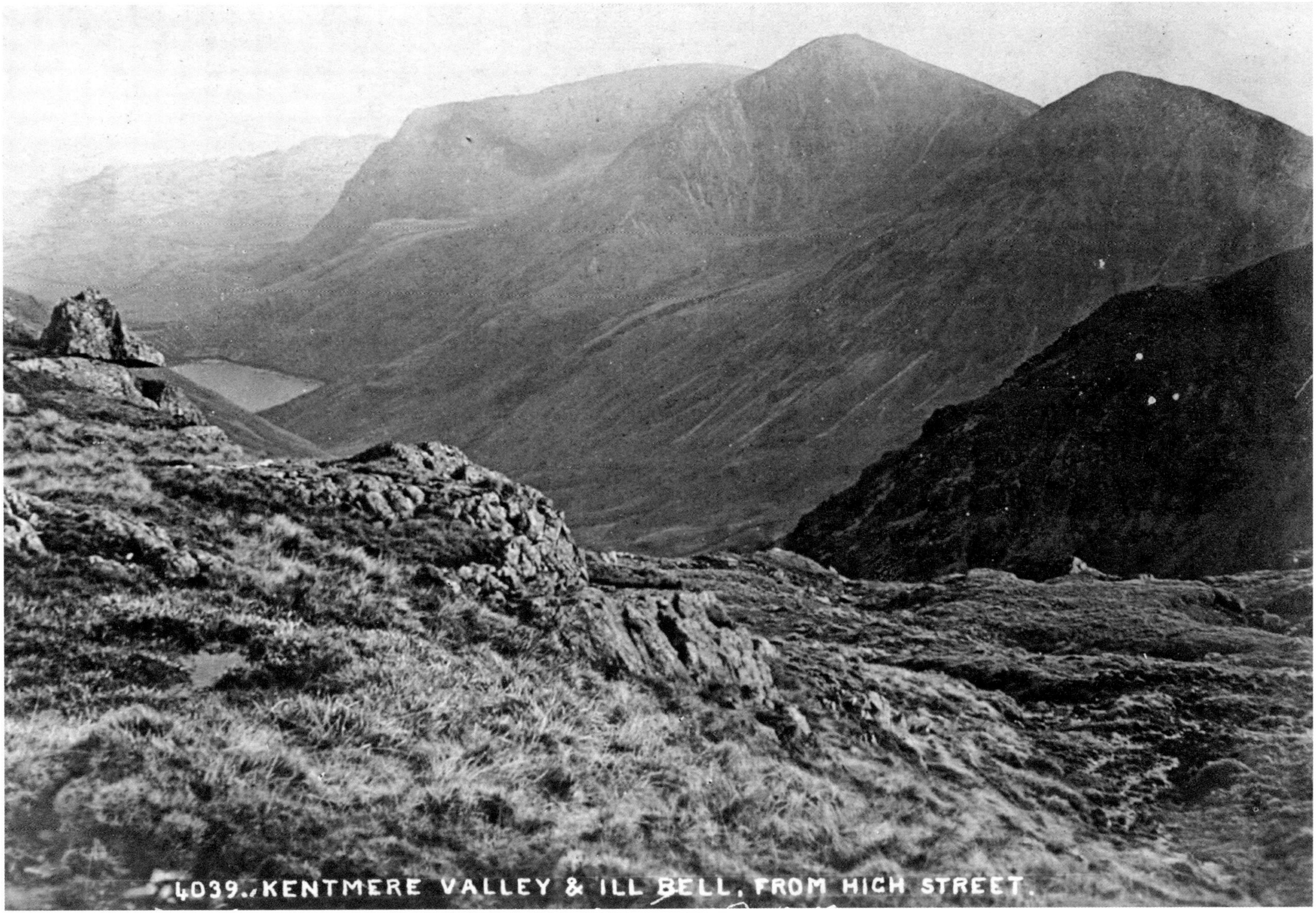
4039. KENTMERE VALLEY & ILL BELL. FROM HIGH STREET.

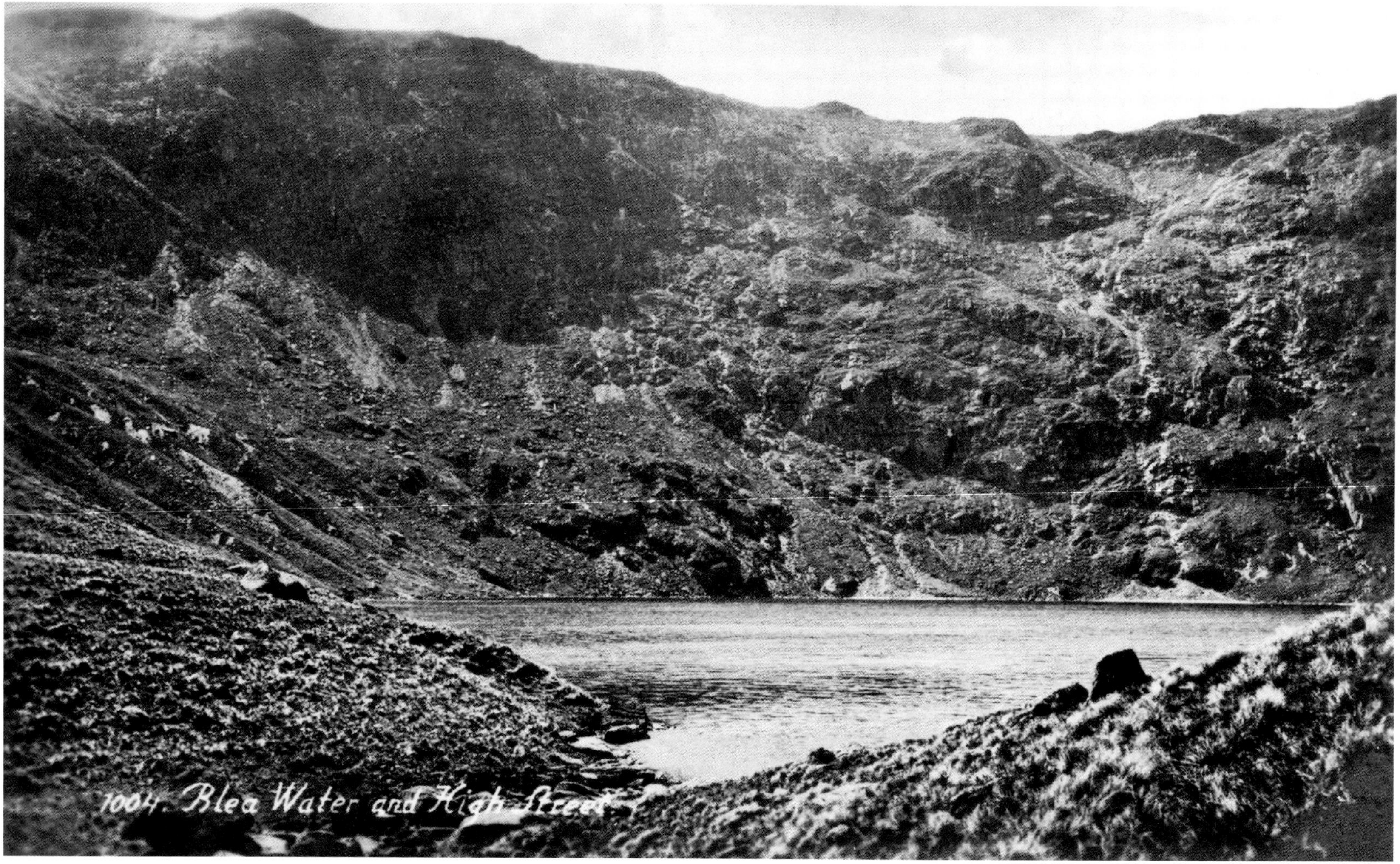

There are two tarns high up on Mardale Head. Blea Water, dark and forbidding, is, at just over 200 feet, the deepest tarn in the Lake District. It is a mysterious place, and has been designated a Site of Special Scientific Interest. Half a mile away, separated by Piot Crag and near the pass itself, lies Small Water, a delightful mountain tarn with a shingly beach. There are some stone shelters near the path, their builders unknown, but they perhaps afforded some protection against extreme weather. Becks from both tarns trickle into Haweswater.

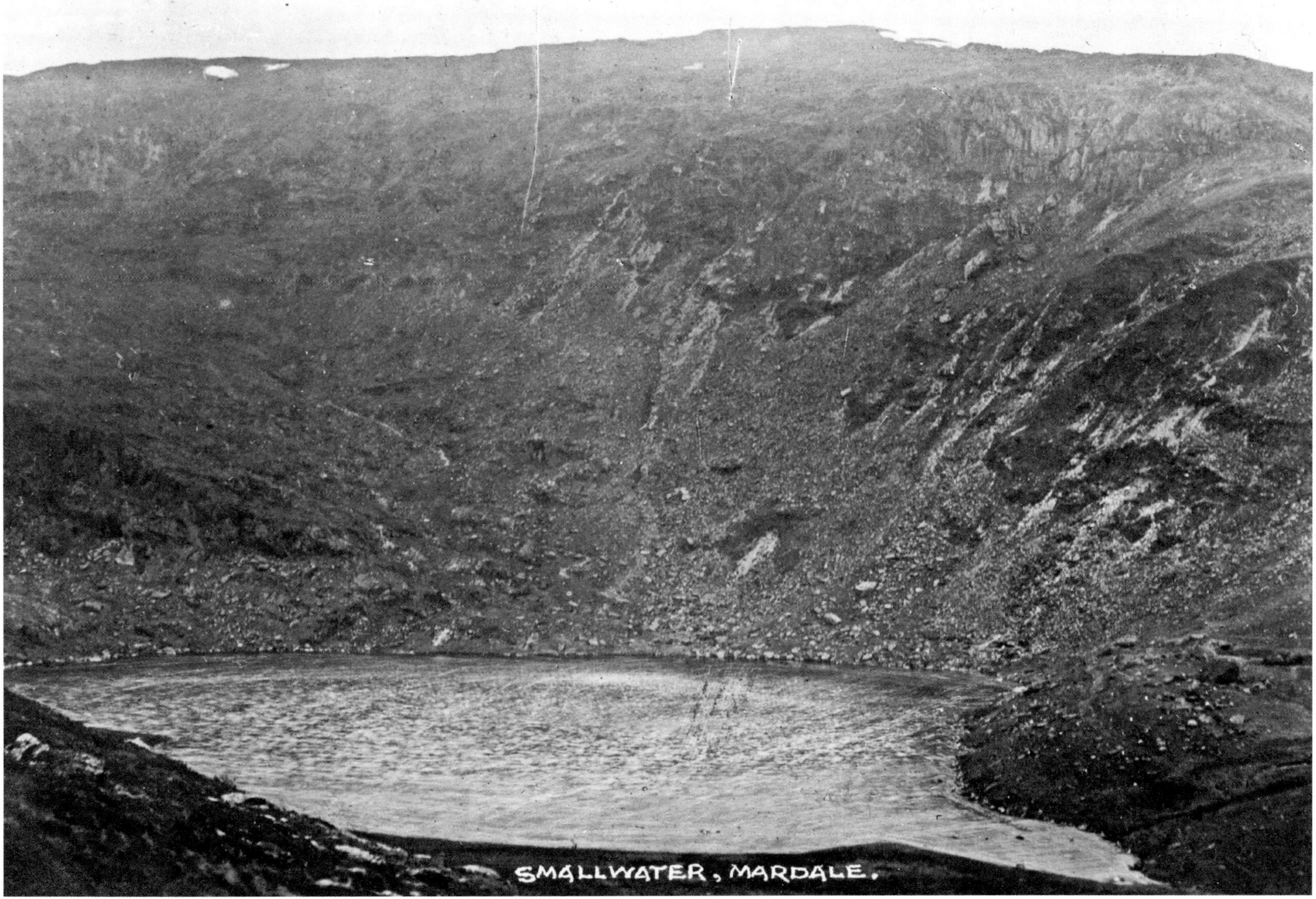
SMALLWATER, MARDALE.

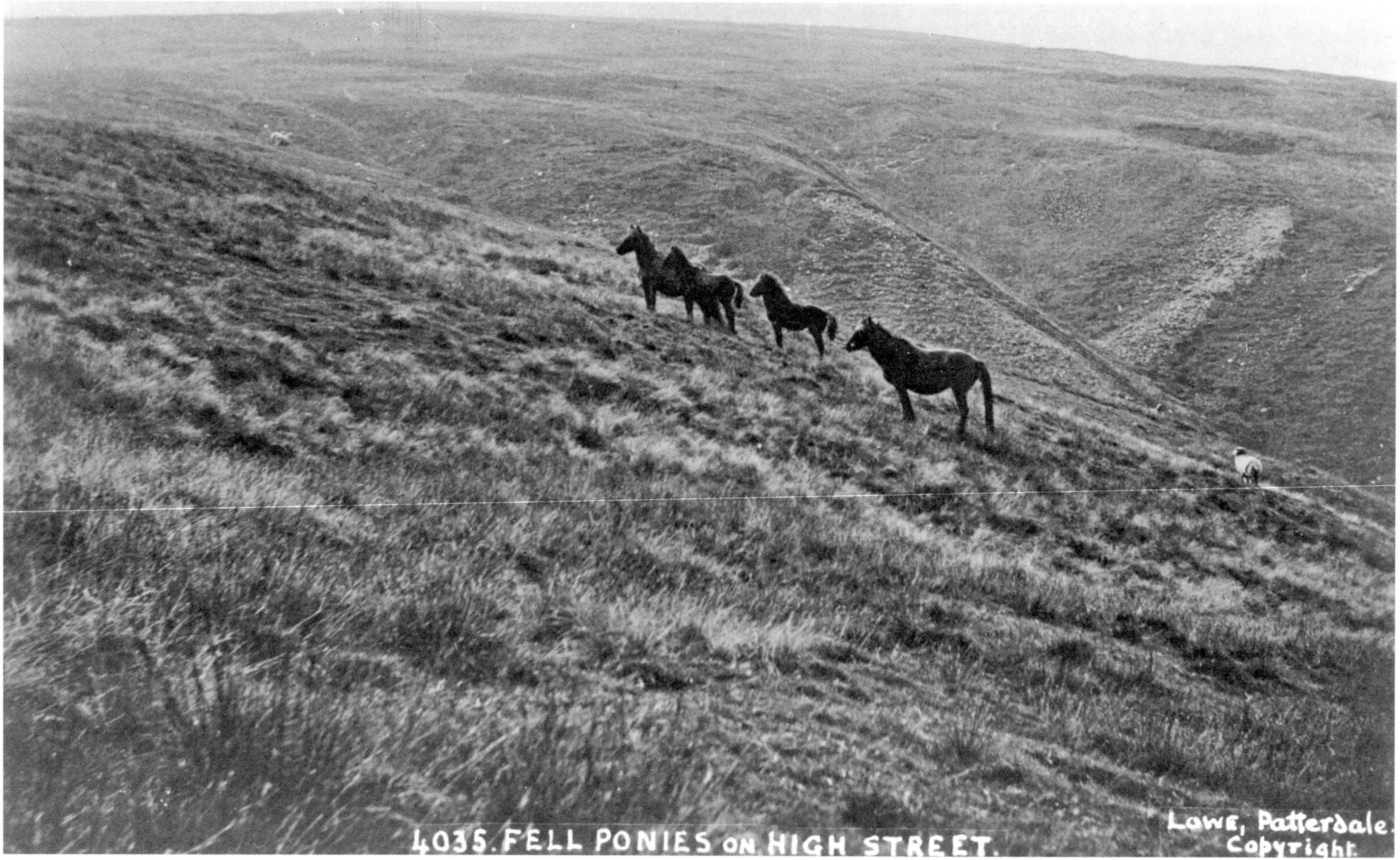

In the summer of 1995 I drove to the car park at Mardale Head and walked up to Nan Bield Pass. It was a lovely summer's morning, but as I neared the summit I became enveloped in thick mist. I slowly edged along the path which leads to High Street when, suddenly, I was surrounded by a group of fell ponies. Fortunately, they were more startled that I was and they soon scattered into the mist. I continued along the path, then I found myself in bright sunshine again, leaving me wondering if it had really happened!

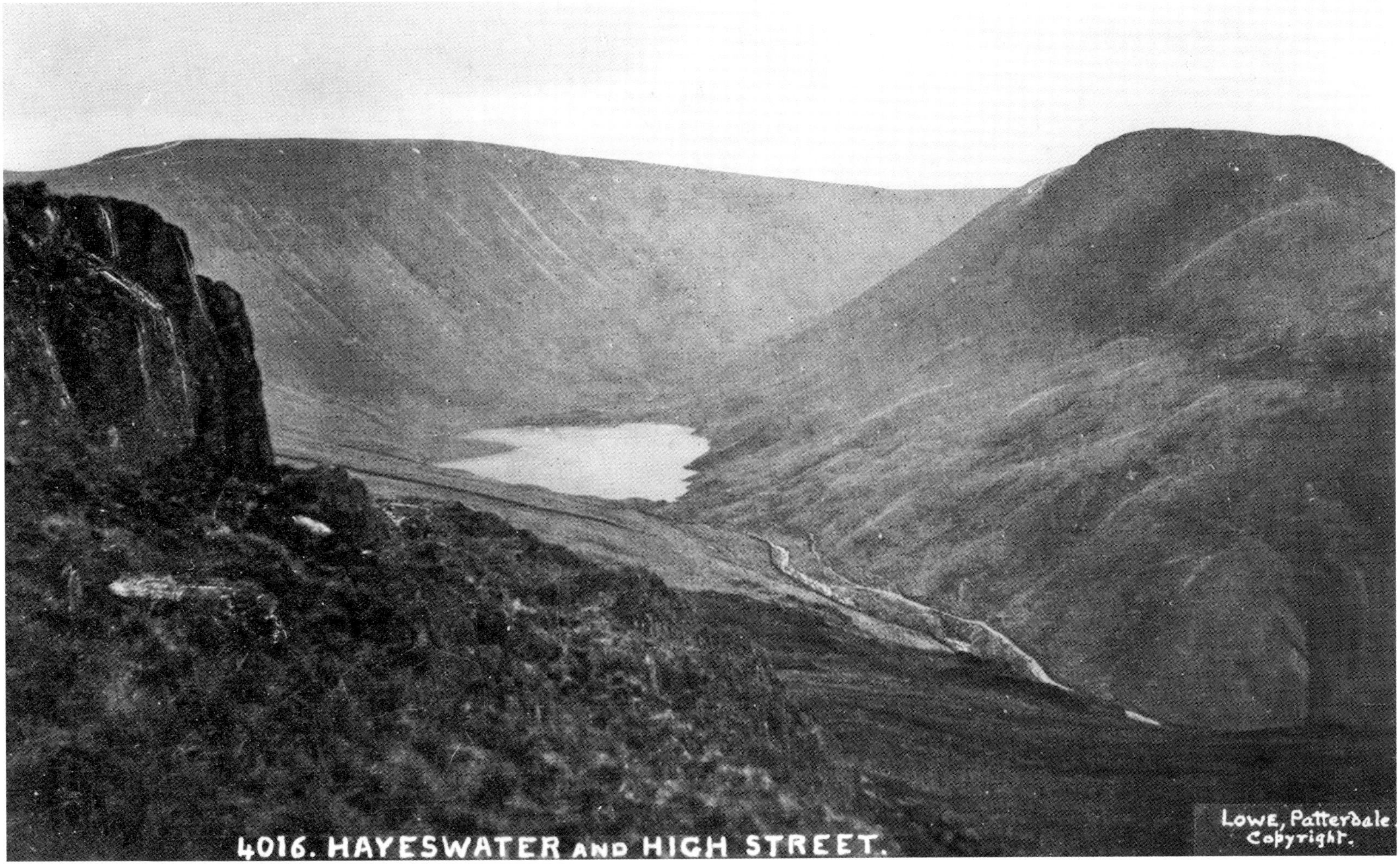

West of High Street, situated about one mile south-east of the hamlet of Hartsop in the Patterdale Valley, lies the small lake called Hayeswater, as shown on this Lowe of Patterdale card. Not to be confused with its larger neighbour Haweswater, this natural lake can be found at an elevation of 1,400 feet, and just over a century ago it was converted into a reservoir to serve the town of Penrith. This is quite a remote location, but one which will be familiar to Coast-to-Coast walkers!

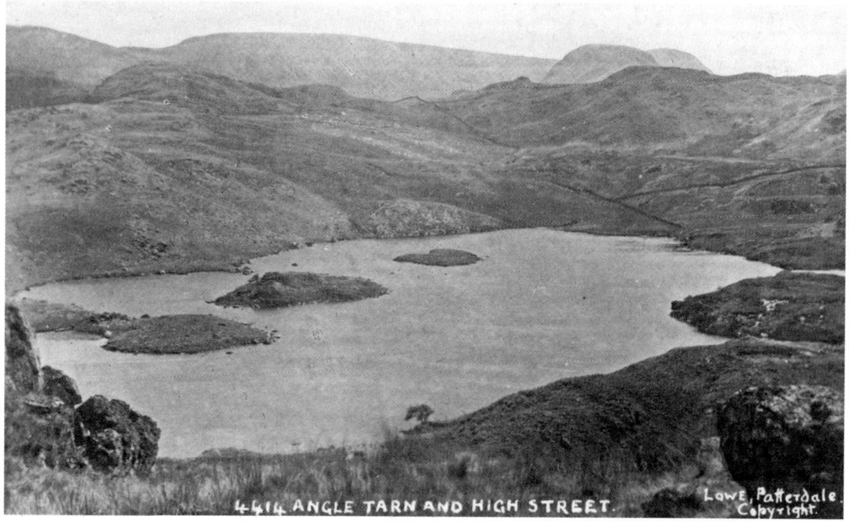

4414. ANGLE TARN AND HIGH STREET.

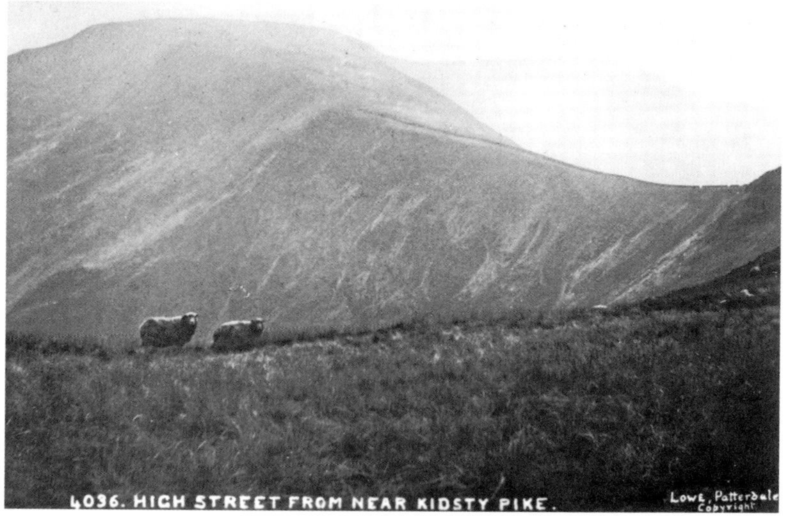

4036. HIGH STREET FROM NEAR KIDSTY PIKE.

These views may be seen by walkers today, but they would have been familiar sights to Roman soldiers 2,000 years ago. They are to be found high above the western side of the Mardale Valley. Peaceful Angle Tarn, an ideal location for a picnic on a nice day, lies above the ascent from Patterdale; soon afterwards, High Street is reached. This flat plateau has been used as a transit route since Roman times. In more recent times it was used by local shepherds and farmers for recreational purposes, being known to locals as "Racecourse Hill". The path winds on to Kidsty Pike, which at 2,560 feet is the highest point in the Mardale Valley and the highest point on the Coast-to-Coast Walk.

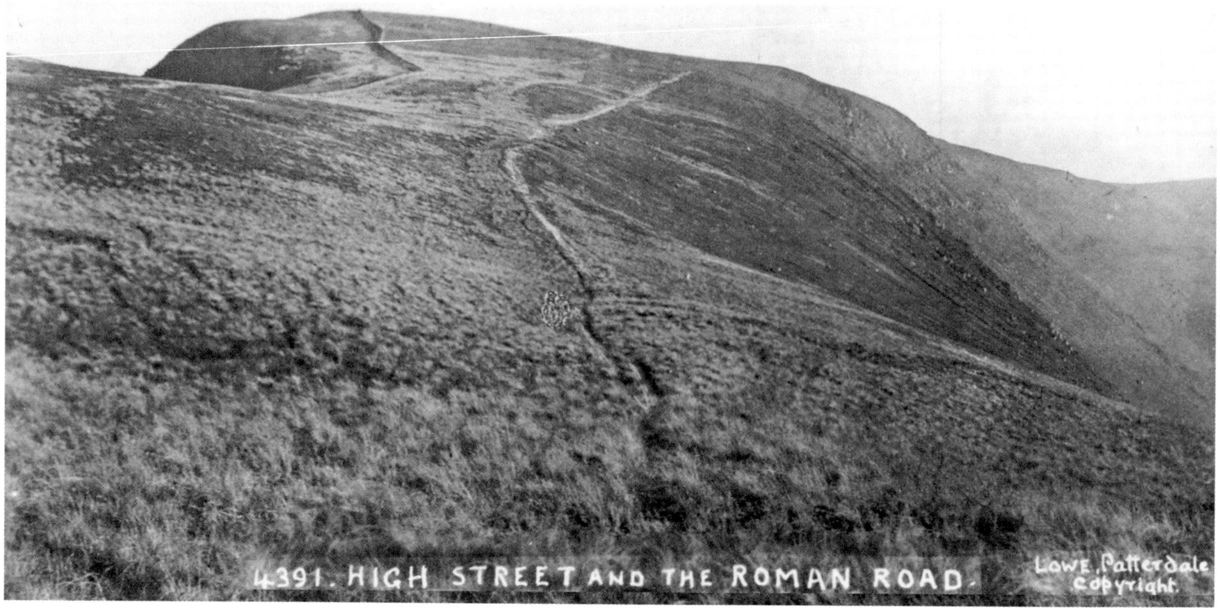

4391. HIGH STREET AND THE ROMAN ROAD.

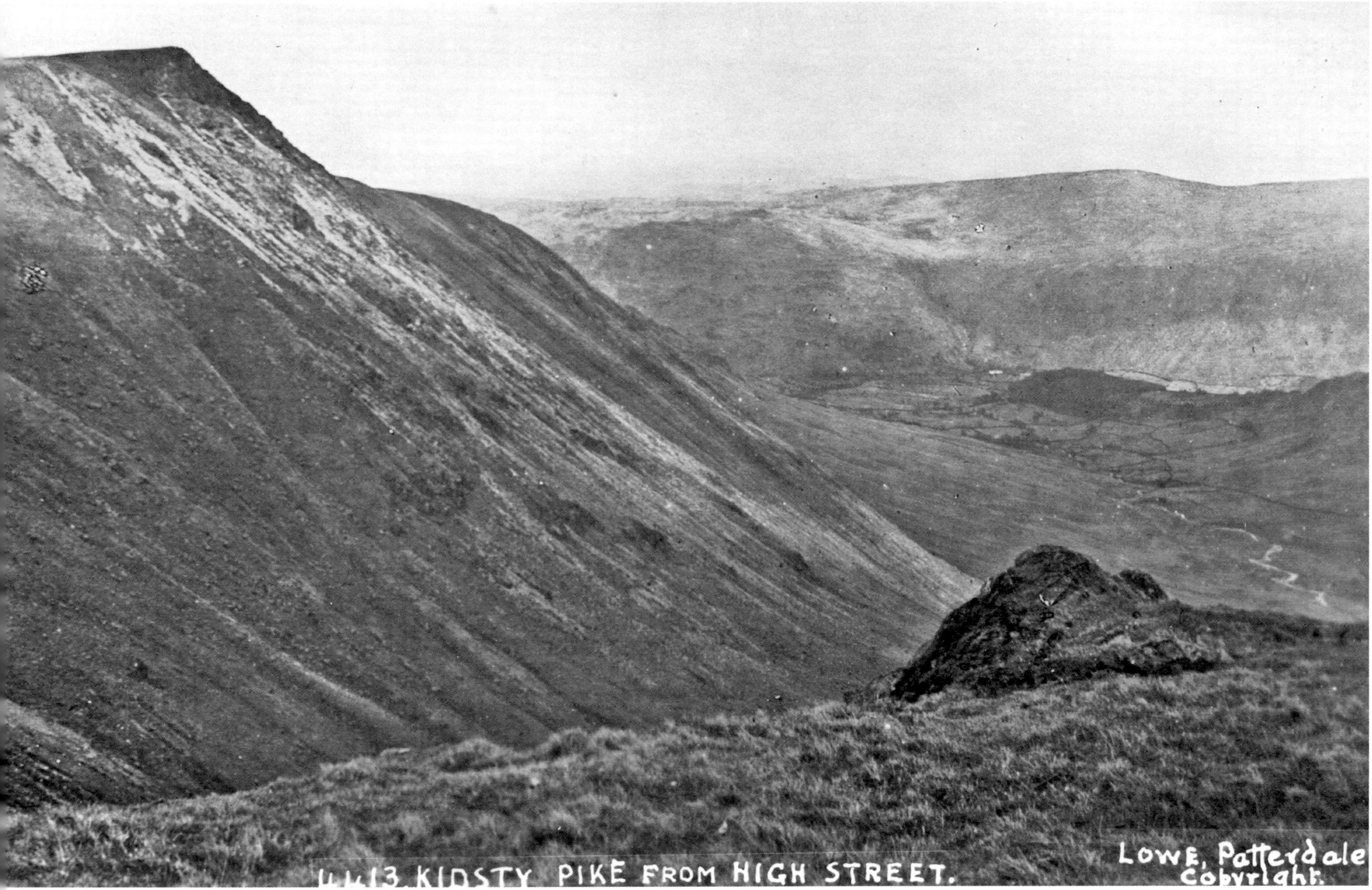
4413. KIDSTY PIKE FROM HIGH STREET.
LOWE, Patterdale
Copyright.

The great charm of Mardale resides in its becks, gills and waterfalls. Fortunately, the creation of the reservoir did not interfere with any of them and in some ways the building of a new road and development of new paths and bridleways have afforded the visitor better access to them. The views on this page show some of the better-known water features in the valley - Thornthwaite Force in the north, Measand Beck on the western side of the valley, and Bleawater Falls near Nan Bield Pass.

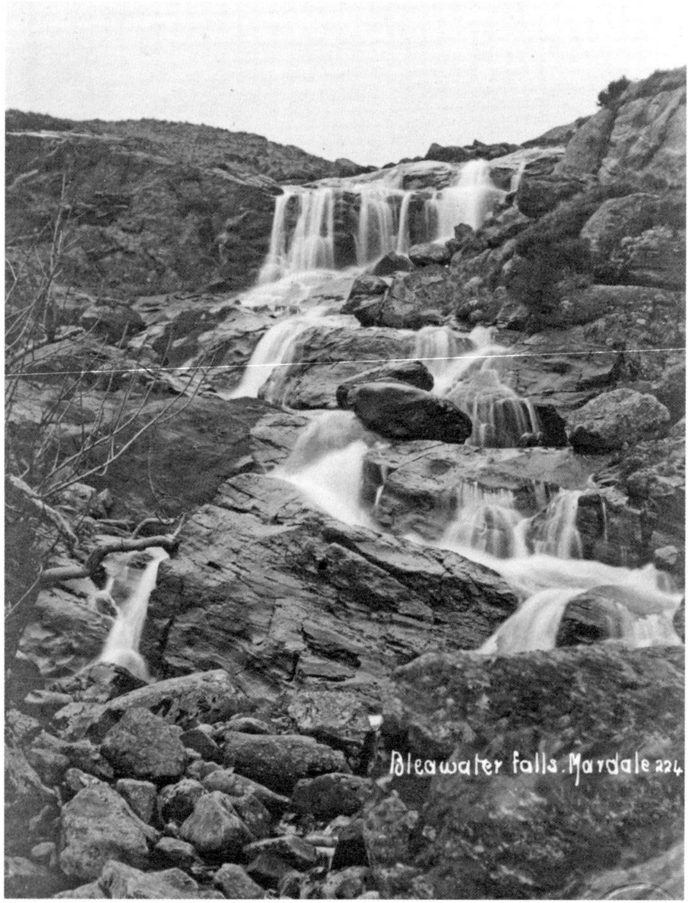

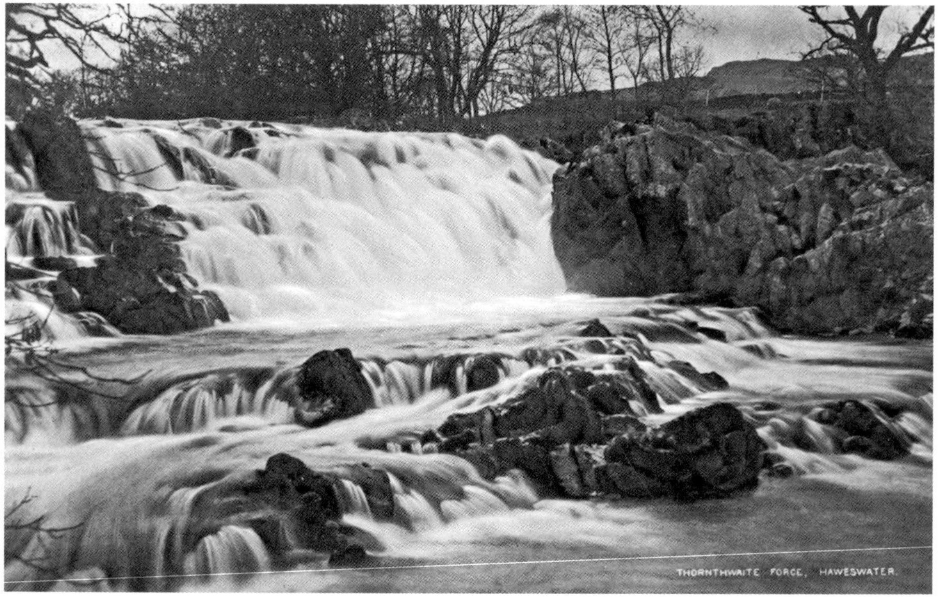

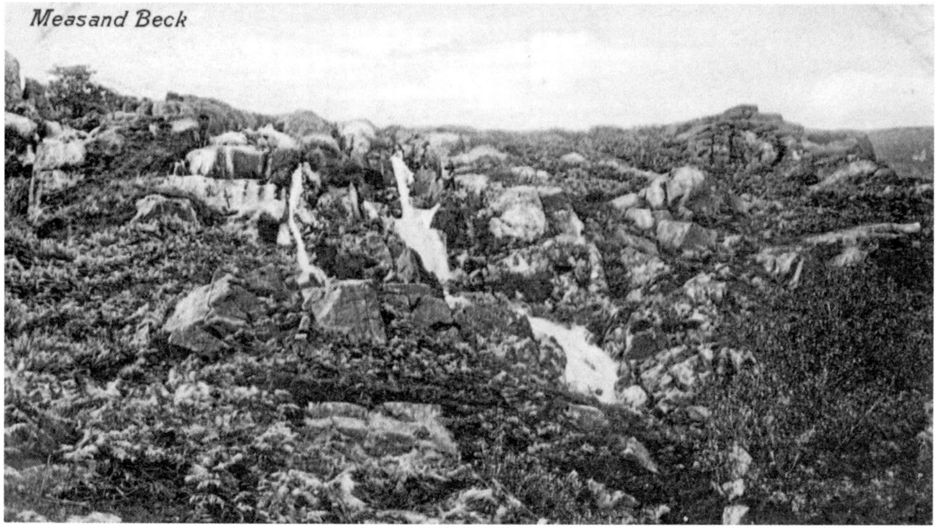

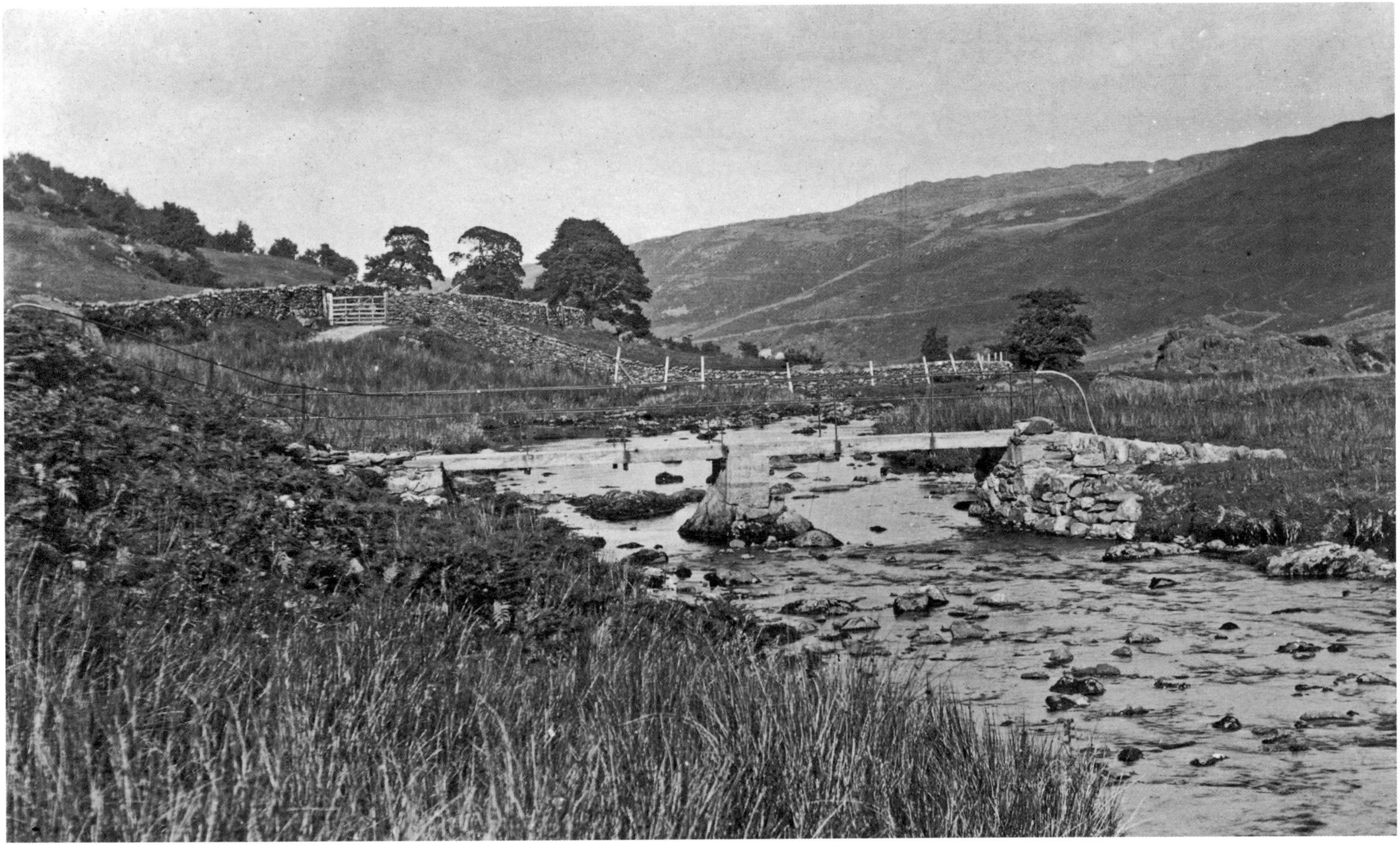

The first burial at Mardale Church took place in 1729. Prior to that time the dead were strapped to the back of horses and carried via the "Corpse Road", a pathway on the eastern side of the valley, over Mardale Common into Swindale and on to Shap, a distance of some eight miles. Legend tells of a wicked local man who had died and as his coffin was being carried to Shap for burial, the young horse bolted in a thunderstorm and roamed the fells for three months! Eventually the horse was captured, and the poor man buried. Swindale is a pleasant little valley, about 2 1/2 miles long and surrounded by craggy fells. The valley fields are fairly flat and fertile and several farms once existed here.

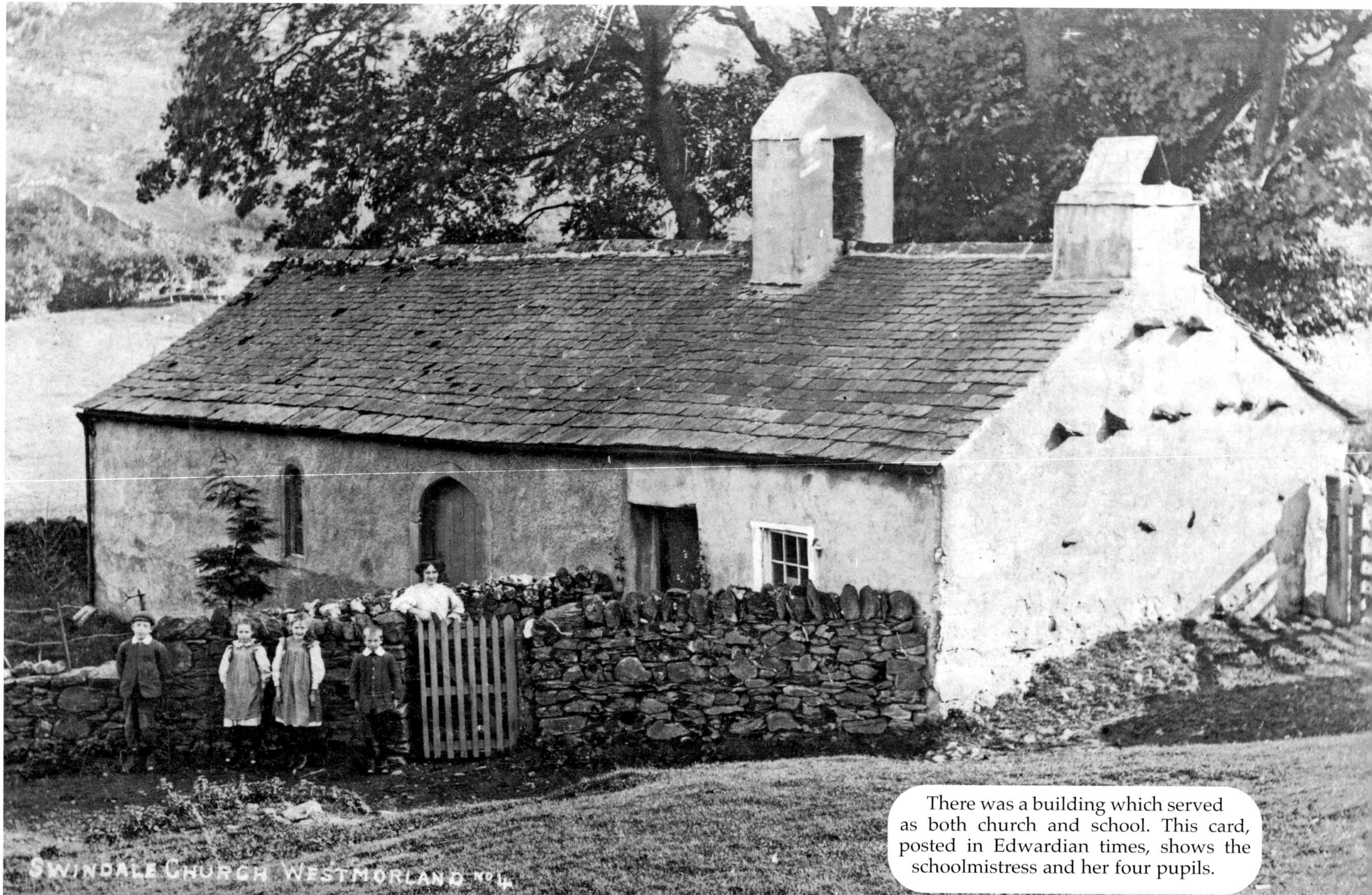

There was a building which served as both church and school. This card, posted in Edwardian times, shows the schoolmistress and her four pupils.

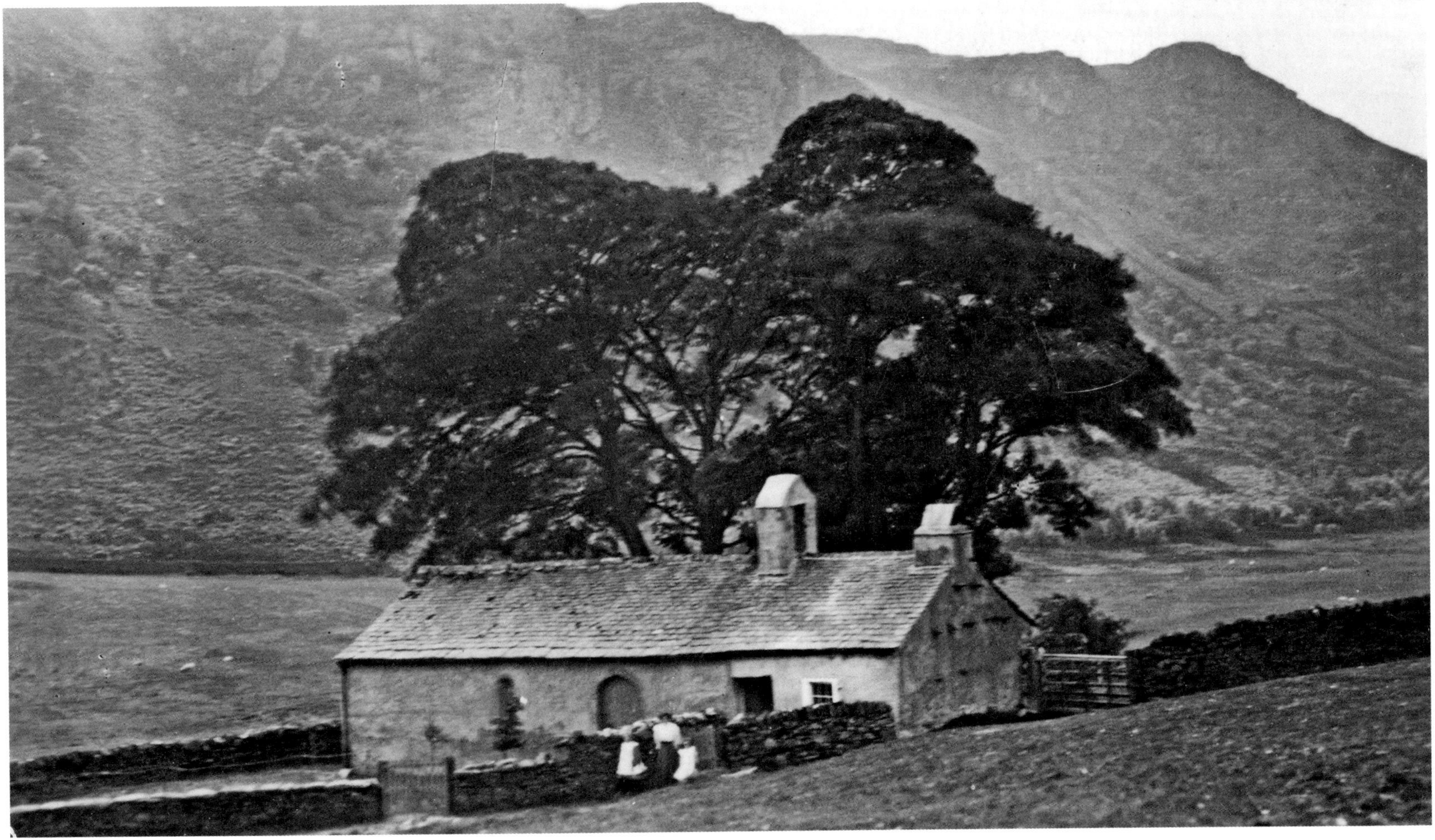

Here is a later view of Swindale Church and School, posted in 1936. The pupil numbers seem to have fallen by 50%! Part of the message reads: "A congregation of 6 is considered good. Service once a month. It is a lovely little valley..." This postcard was sent to a Miss... in London. Oddly enough I found another copy of this card several years later; posted in 1937, it had been written by the same gentleman to a different Miss... in London, reminding her of "our special place"! Manchester Corporation had planned to create another reservoir in Swindale Valley, but it never happened. The valley, however, continued to decline and the church-cum-school fell into ruin. By the 1990s there was only one working farm left. I often wonder whether Mardale would have suffered a similar slow decline had the reservoir not been built.

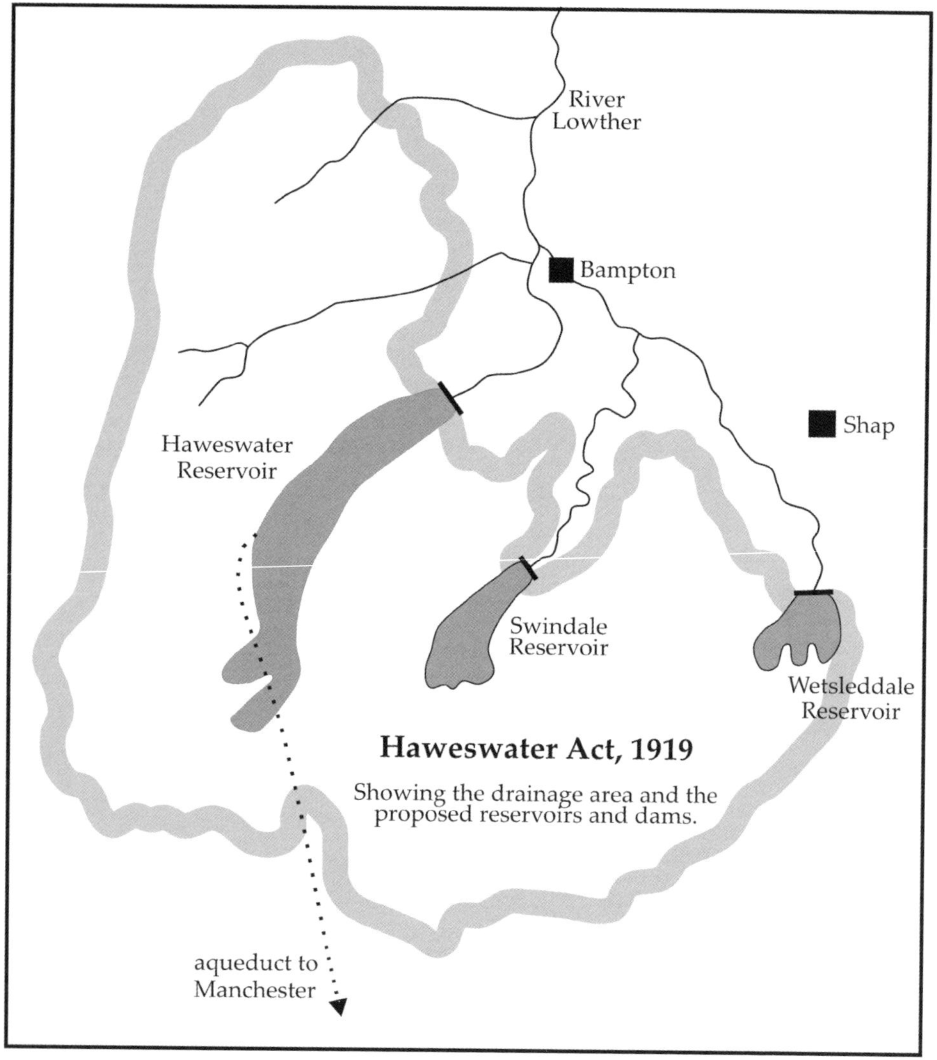

As the large industrial cities of Victorian Britain grew rapidly, fresh sources of water were needed. At one point, there was talk of supplying London via a lengthy aqueduct from Ullswater, Thirlmere and Haweswater. Then, in the 1890s, it looked as though both Manchester and Liverpool would draw their water from those lakes. In the event, Liverpool turned to North Wales and Manchester was left alone to bid for the Lake District. Thirlmere Reservoir was created at this time, but it quickly became obvious that another source was needed and Mancunian eyes turned to Haweswater, the highest and remotest lake in the Lake District. In 1919 Manchester Corporation secured the Haweswater Act, which gave the go-ahead for the creation of a new reservoir from the lake and a large catchment area. The Act also provided for the development of subsidiary reservoirs in Swindale and Wetsleddale Valleys, and that water from all of these new reservoirs would be sent via a 73-mile long aqueduct to Manchester. Work began on the Haweswater dam in 1930. The Wetsleddale reservoir was completed in 1966; as yet Swindale remains untouched. After several years of planning, a large official party from Manchester arrived at Penrith Station in July 1925. They travelled via an assortment of vehicles to Mardale, had afternoon tea at the Dun Bull, then returned to Penrith for dinner. It was agreed that the lake be increased from 2 1/2 to four miles long, and the water level raised by 96 feet. The chairman of the Waterworks Committee, Sir Edward Holt, seeking to allay fears that the reservoir would destroy the natural beauty of the valley stated, "I think there will be no more charming spot in the country than Haweswater when we have finished it. It is our intention to improve the appearance of the whole surroundings because we shall do as we have done at Thirlmere. In my opinion Haweswater is presently very much over-rated. It will be more beautiful in years to come."

By 1929 plans for the Haweswater project had been finalised. Apart from the dam itself, a new road was to be constructed on the east side of the valley and a replacement hotel built part way along it. A series of aqueducts and tunnels would complete the work. Needless to say, a huge amount of manpower would be needed, navvies and skilled workers, single men and married men with their families. For these, a "model village" of small bungalows with cast-iron frames would be built on the fellside at Burnbanks, at the entrance to the valley.

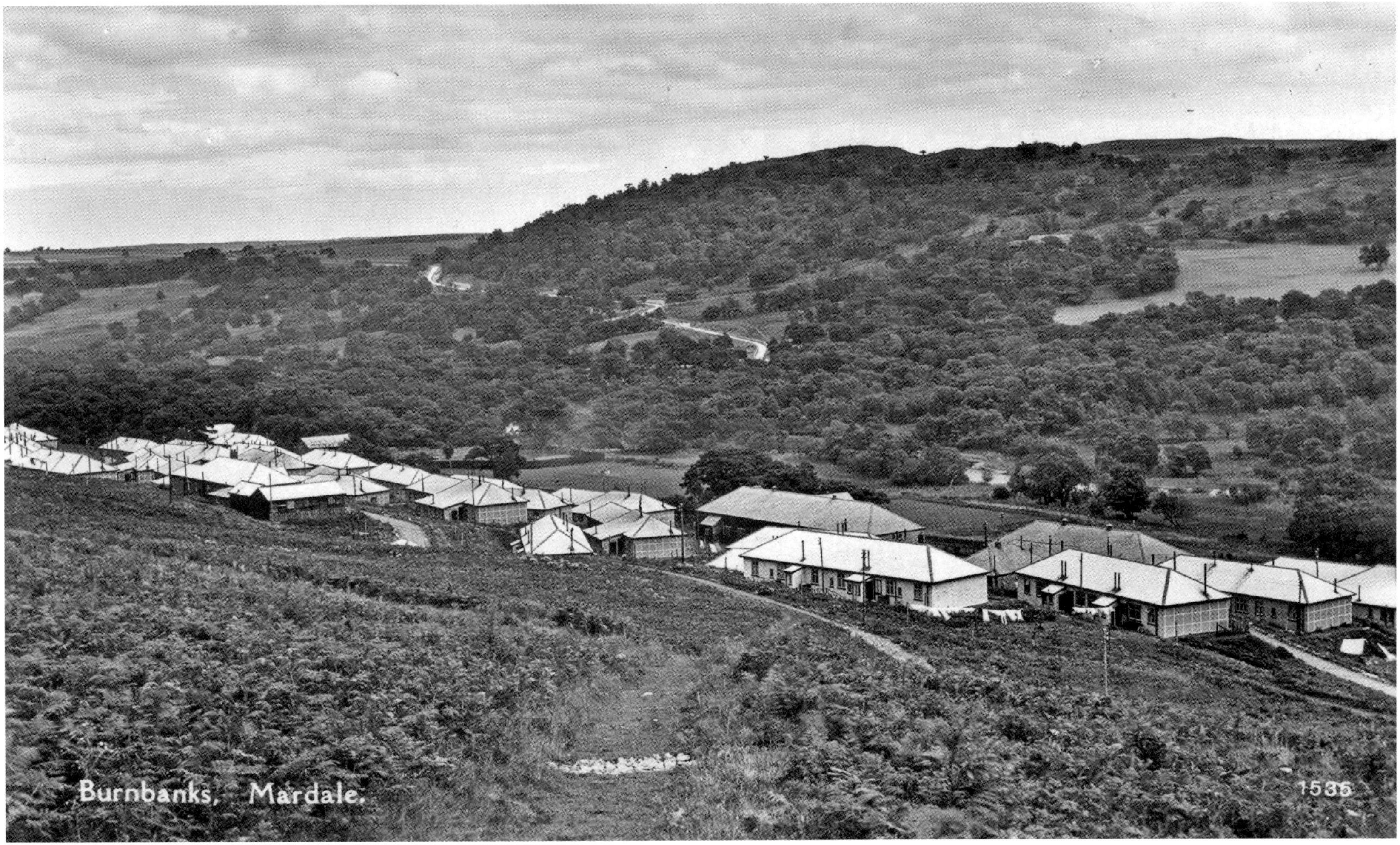

Construction began in September 1929 and the village was completed before the end of the year. There were four different kinds of accommodation - communal dwellings for a "hut keeper" and his family and for up to thirteen single men, and family bungalows with one, two or three bedrooms. Burnbanks was like a modern version of Saltaire or New Lanark, as many amenities - recreation and dance halls, a canteen, sports facilities, a dispensary, a shop, allotments, etc - were built. The Daily Mail dubbed the new settlement "Aquaville"! The workers mainly came from the Manchester area or from West Cumberland. By the beginning of 1931, 400 workers and their families were living in this unusual Lakeland settlement.

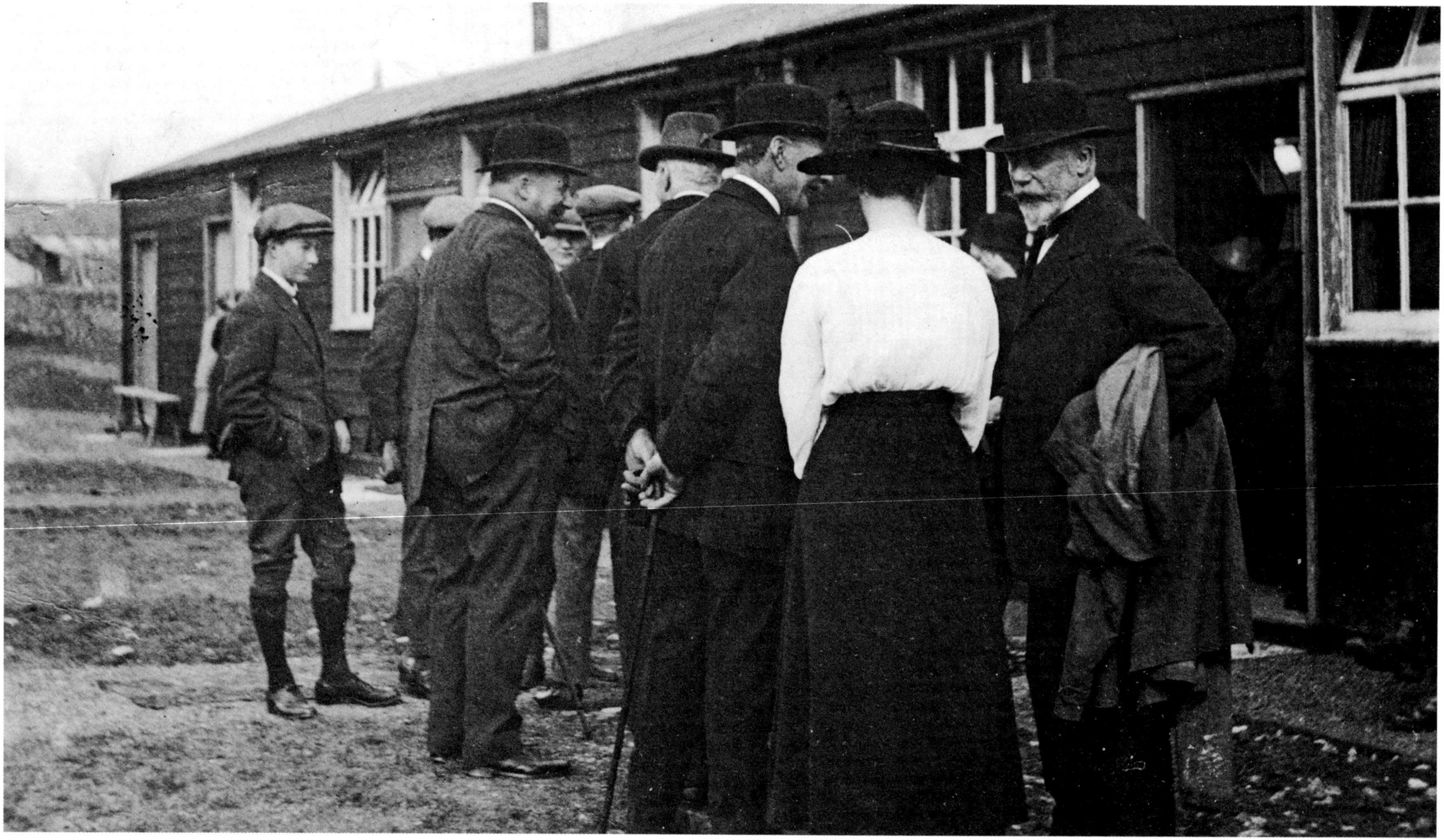

The dam was completed by 1941 and by the following year most of the valley had become a lake. Part of Burnbanks village was dismantled, as temporary buildings were desperately needed during the war, but some of the settlement was retained to accommodate the workers who would maintain the dam and the Haweswater Estate. Trees were planted between the remaining houses and the dam. After the war, contractors replaced some of the workers and some of the houses were abandoned. The arrival of golden eagles in Riggindale revived the community, as more accommodation was needed for RSPB personnel, but as the millenium approached the settlement was sold to a private firm and the old buildings were dismantled and scrapped. New bungalows were, however, constructed, and so Burnbanks lives on.

Work on building the dam began in 1930, but was postponed because of the national financial crisis. A smaller scheme was considered, but in 1934 work began again according to the original design. The dam was to be a hollow-buttress type, unique in Britain. When completed, it would be 96 feet high and approximately 1550 feet long and the reservoir would have a capacity of about 18,600 million gallons. The dam itself would consist of some 40 massive buttress blocks, with six-feet walls and flexible joints to keep it watertight. It was possible to walk through the entire structure, and there was a walkway on the top. Much of the stone for the new dam was quarried in the valley, at levels which would be covered as the water rose. Huge machines known as "Blondins" (after the famous French high wire walker) moved buckets of concrete up and down and across the valley. The picture on the right shows an early stage of the work, and the cables of a Blondin may be seen at the top left corner. The image below shows part of the power station of the dam.

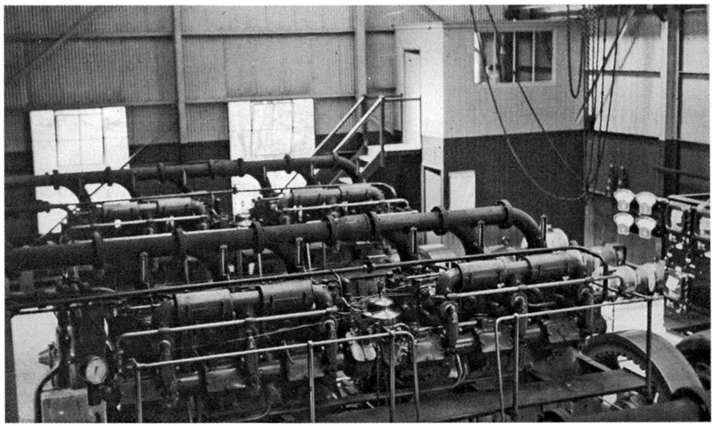

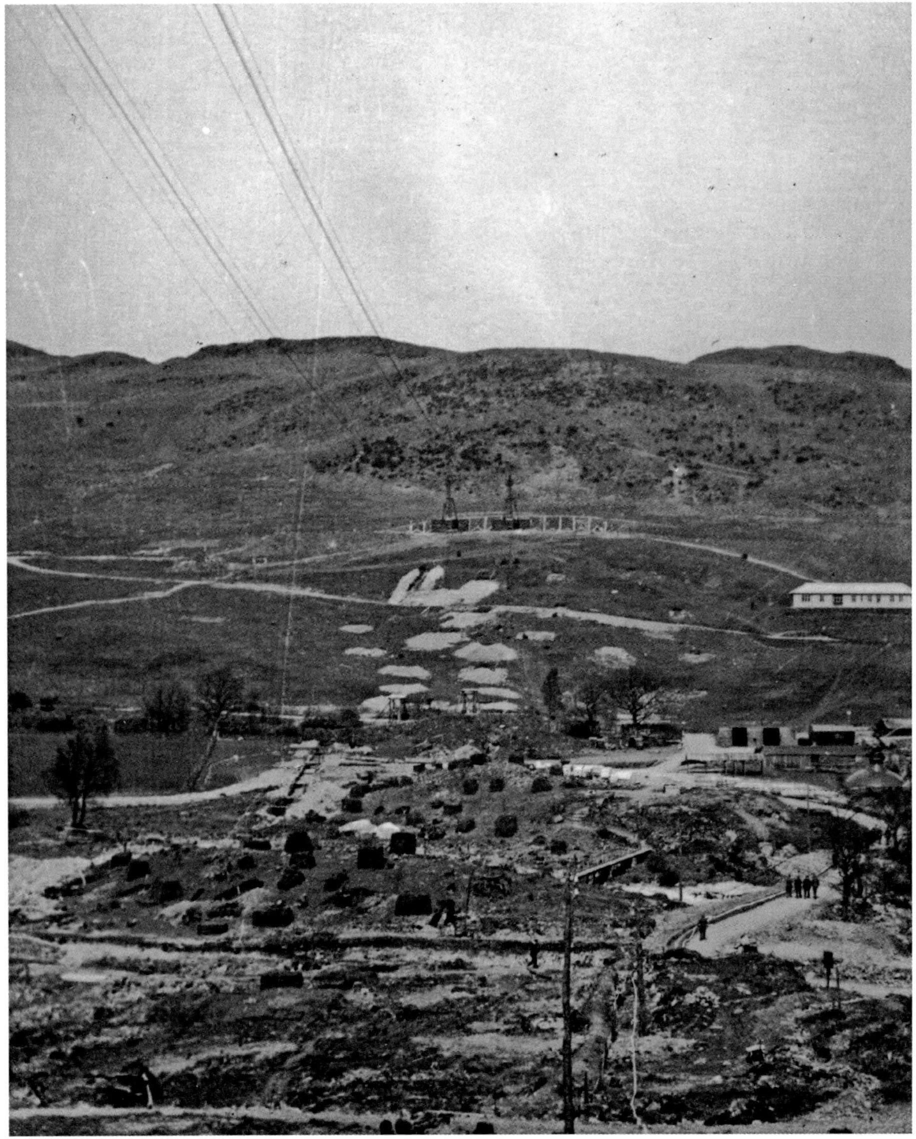

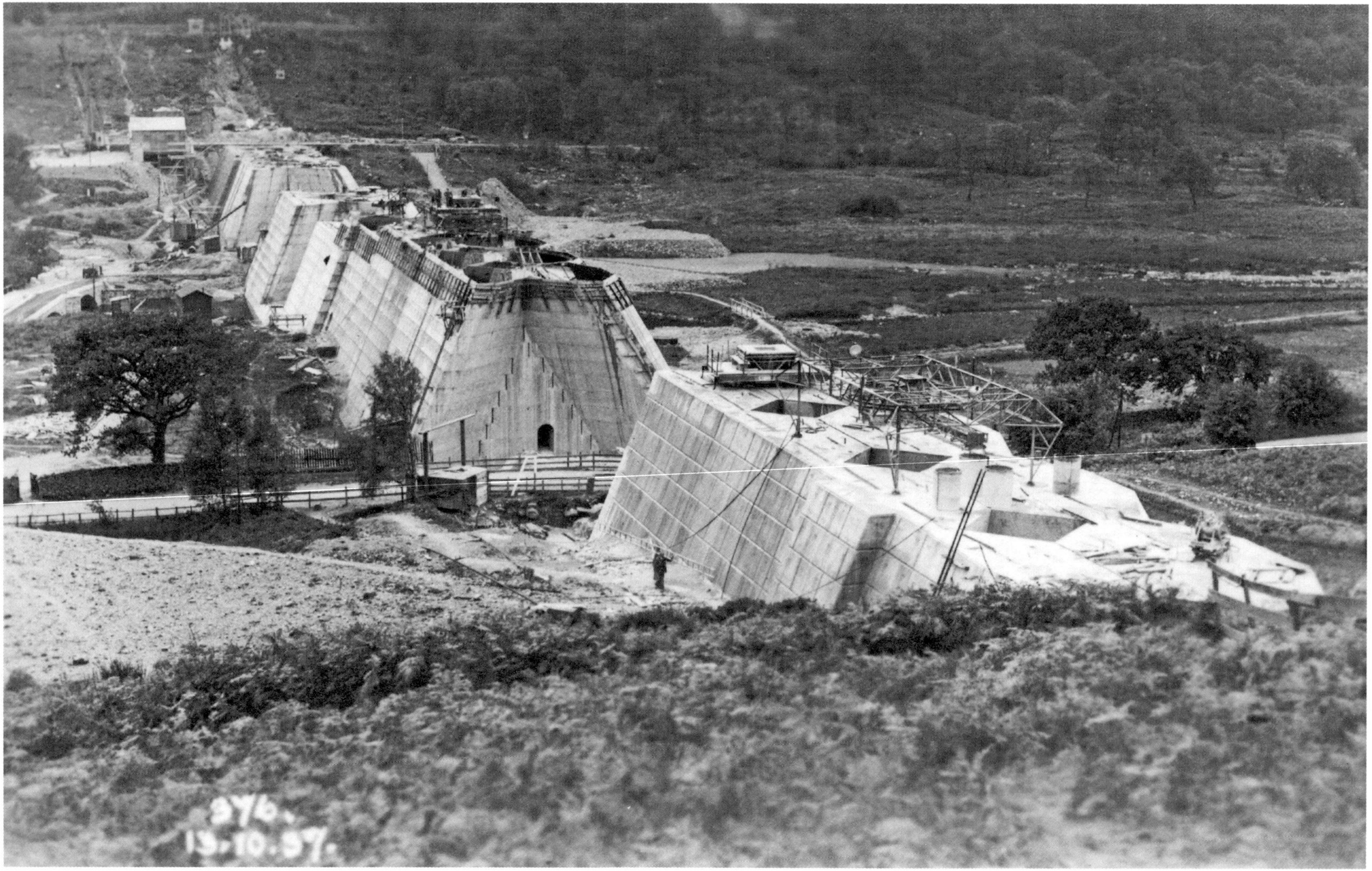

By October 1937 the lower buttresses were almost complete. The Herald, printed at nearby Penrith, told its readers: "From some distance up the old fern-clad, cranesbill-haunted road to Mardale, the white concrete barrier at the lower end of the lake looks like some kind of titanic ship on the slips of the builders…….close to the massive basement there is a suggestion that you are standing at the foot of the Pyramids of Egypt in course of construction."

Left: Work beginning on the upper level of the dam.

Centre: The completed dam.

Bottom: The centre spillway of the dam.

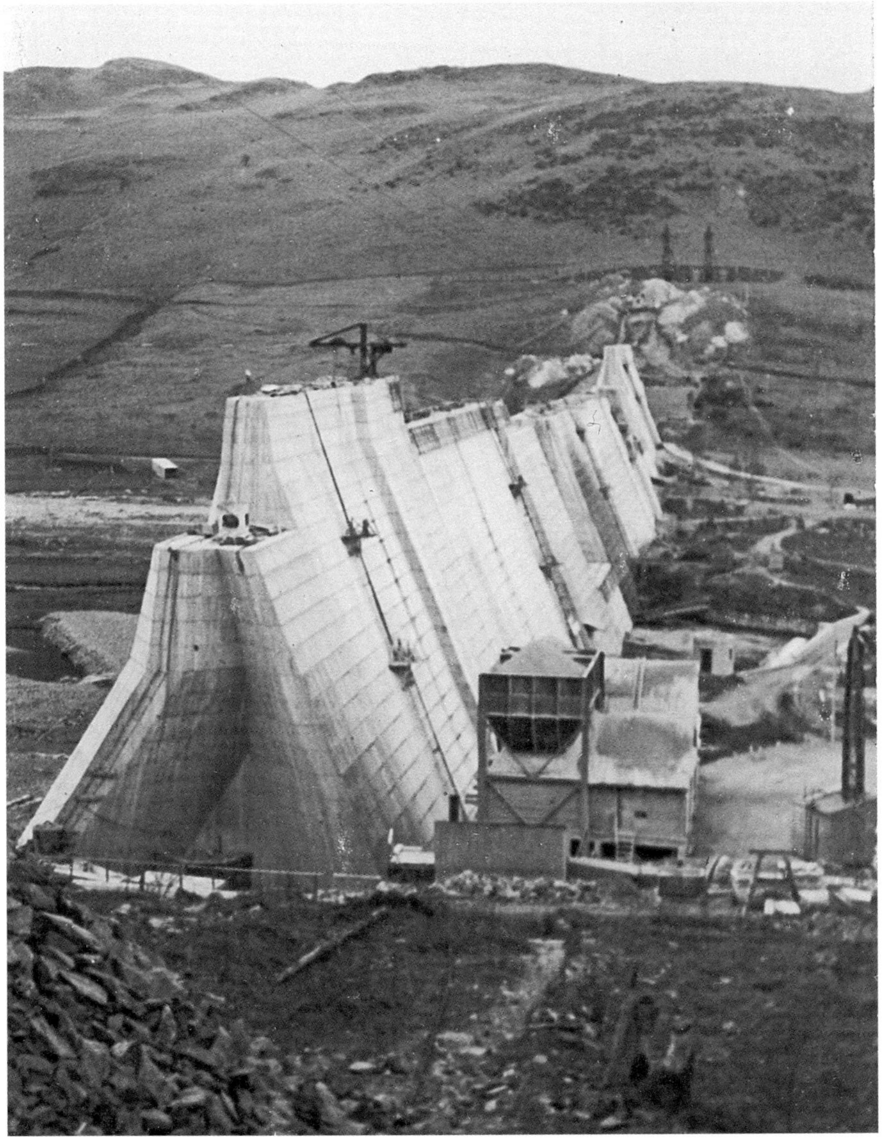

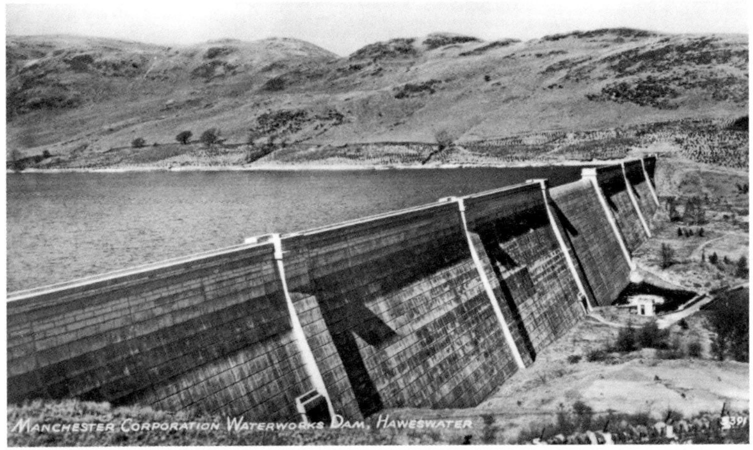

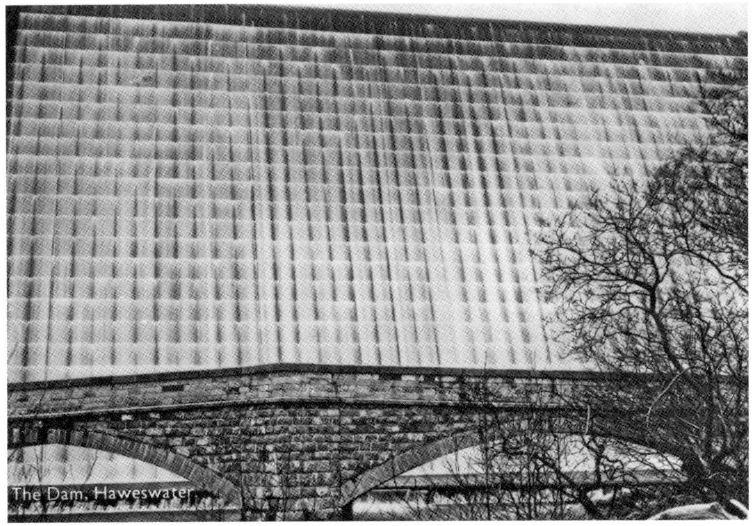

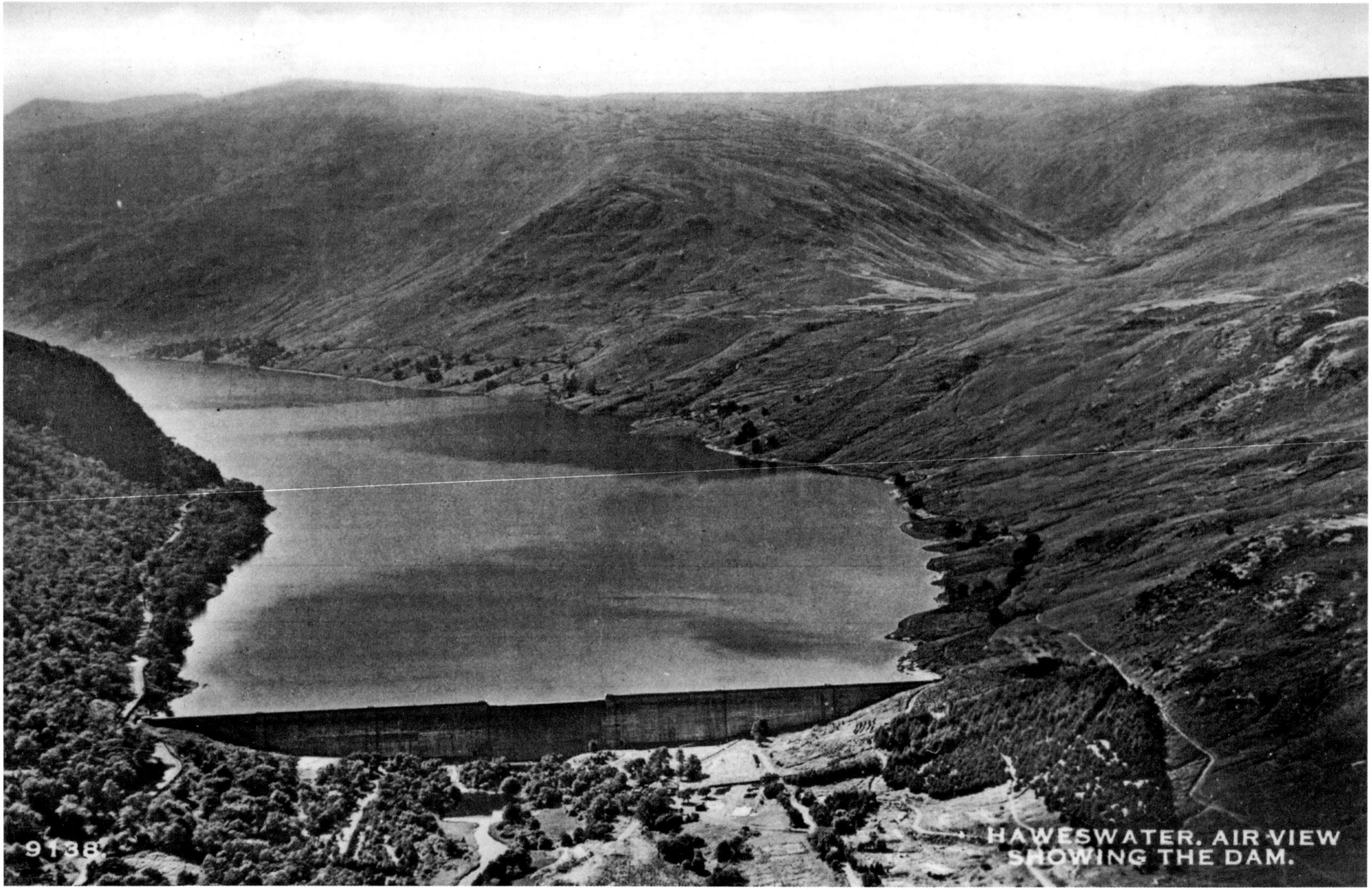

When war broke out in 1939, some of the workers left to join the armed forces, but work continued on the dam and by 1942 it was finished. The Mardale Valley had become a lake

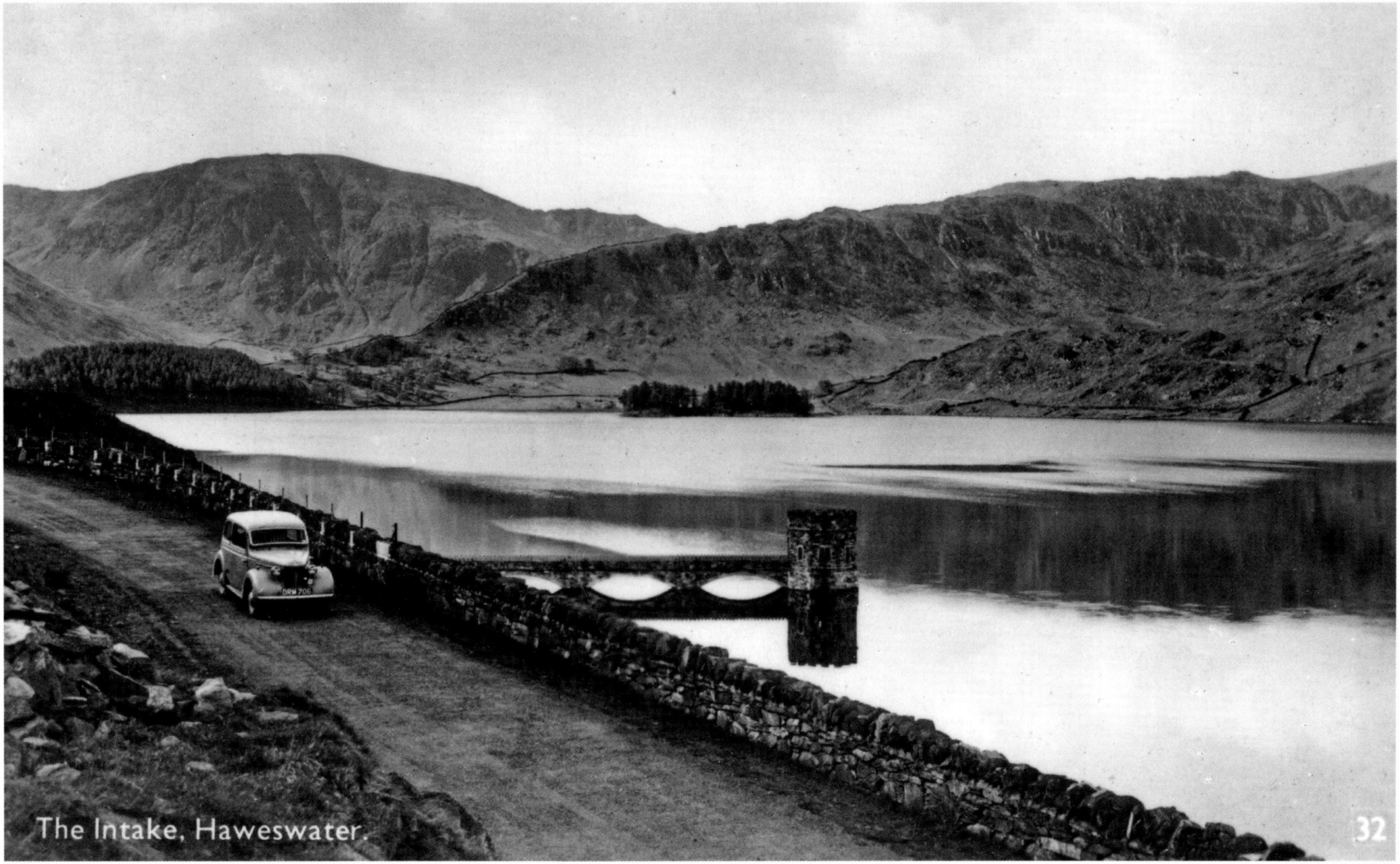

When Holy Trinity Church was dismantled in the late 1930s, its windows and much of its stone were used to build the reservoir's draw-off tower, seen in its early days here. A screen of trees now hide the tower from the road. Water was drawn from the reservoir via an aqueduct in the Mardale Tunnel and was carried by pipeline to Garnett Bridge, where it joined the Thirlmere Aqueduct. Since the war the water supply has been improved by the building of more modern aqueducts.

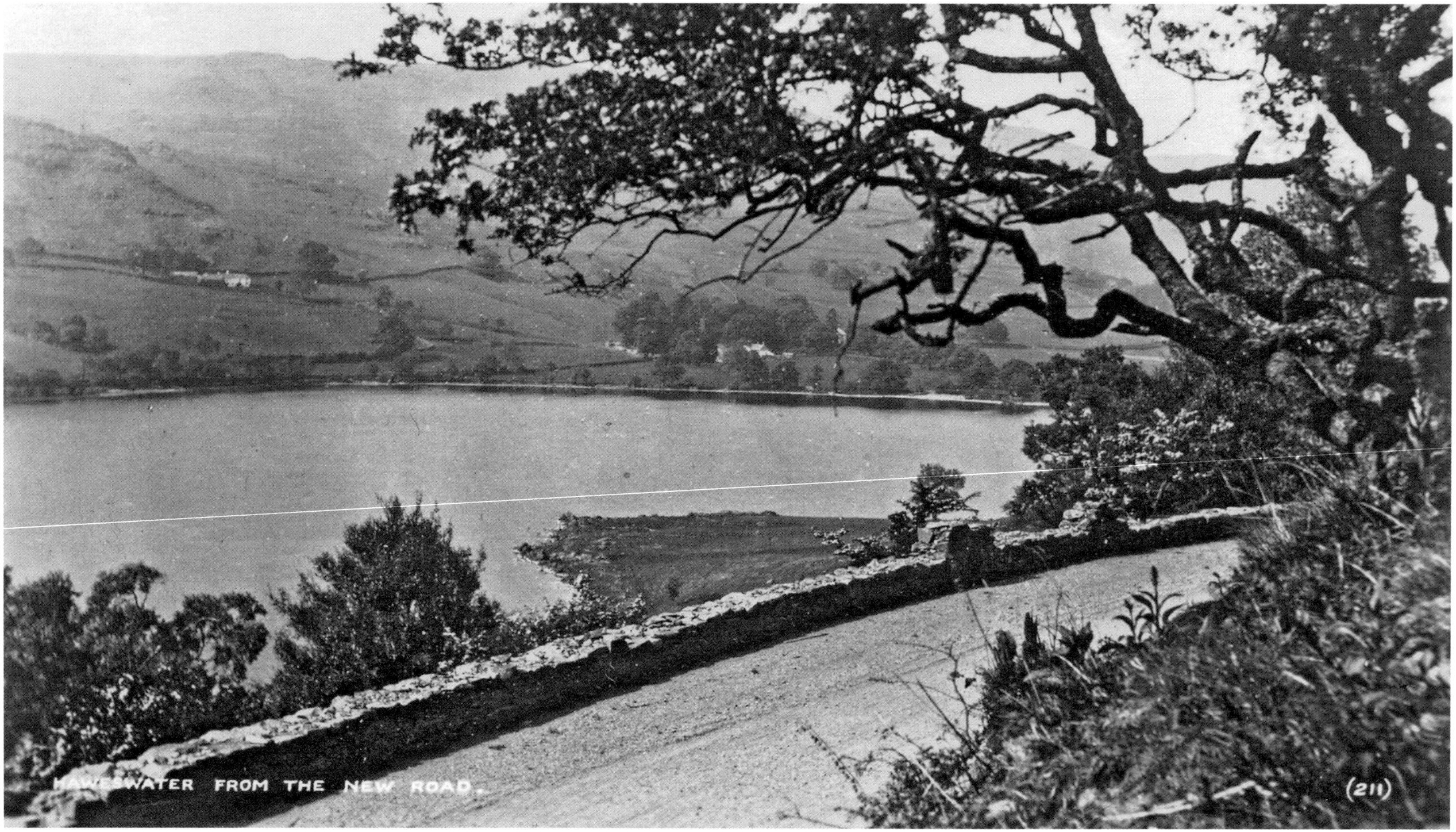

The Haweswater scheme condemned the old, winding road which ran along the west shore of the lake to a watery grave. The planners decided that a new road would be constructed on the opposite side of the lake, running through Naddle Forest to the dalehead. The road, which was made by direct labour between 1929 and 1931, was about 20 feet wide, with immense retaining walls and bridges over the becks. Many people considered that it was too large for the light traffic that was expected, and that it was an ugly scar on the valley side. A footpath was provided on the west side of the reservoir. Another new road, nearly six miles long and composed of reinforced concrete slabs, was built across the moorland to link the building site in the valley to the granite works at Shap. This photograph was taken soon after the new road was built. It shows the road and the views across the valley. The dam was still under construction and the road was high above the lake. Two farms were left standing on the other side.

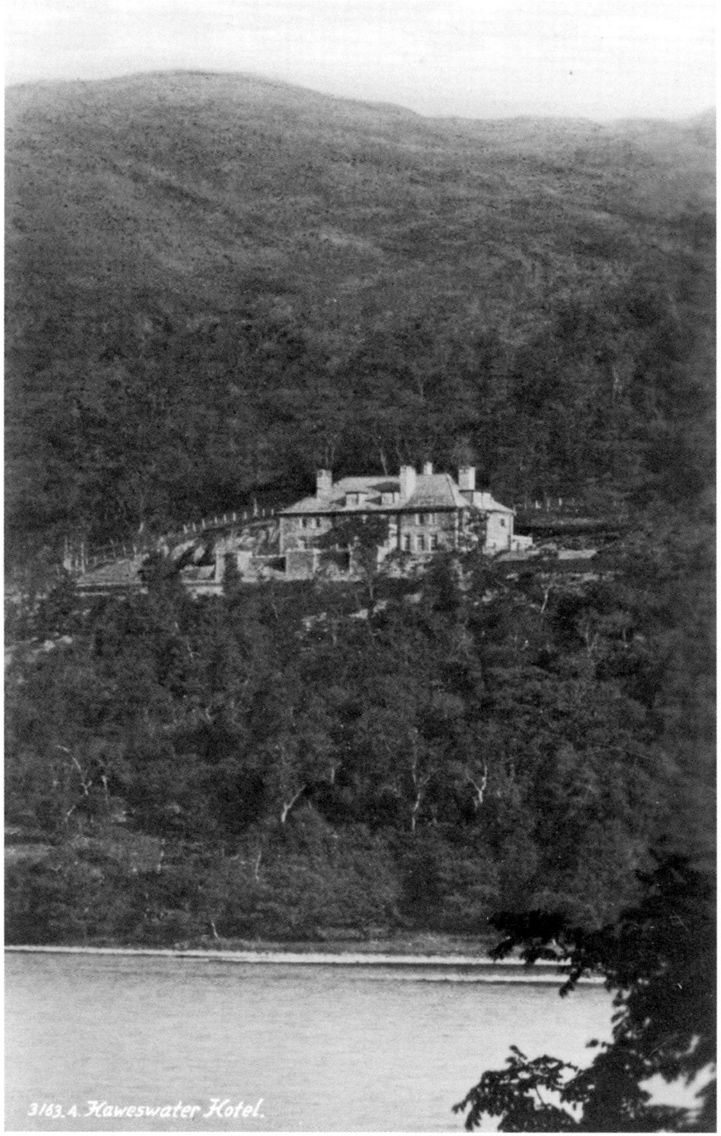

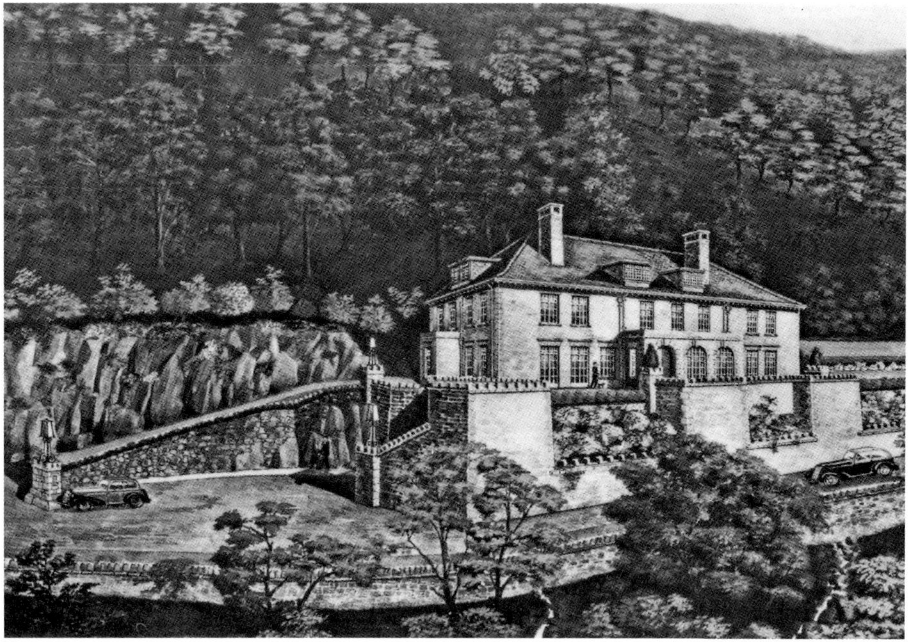

Many people thought that a replacement for the Dun Bull should be built at the dale head, perhaps at the meeting of track ways on the Rigg above the former Chapel Hill settlements, but it was decided that the new hotel would be built on the new road. The site chosen was a kind of shelf below Guerness Woods, about a mile and a half beyond the dam, with extensive views of the lake and background hills. A small pipeline would remove the sewage from the hotel to a point below the dam. There was further disagreement over the design of the new hotel. Many agreed with the Council for the Preservation of Rural England that the hotel ought to be a traditional design, a low whitewashed building similar to the ones that once stood in the valley. The Manchester architects, however, preferred a more modern design with a castellated front and terraced gardens, as shown in the artist's impression. Several years of discussions and arguments resulted in the hotel which stands today. When the hotel opened in 1937, the Penrith *Herald* described the building "Haweswater's Castle of Chillon", and as the photograph on the left shows, the hotel occupied a strangely-elevated position above the lake. Five years later, when the dam had been completed and the waters had risen by 90 feet, the water level was just below the hotel's rock base. The views were magnificent, with a panorama from Harter Fell to High Street and Measand, and guests were spared the sight of the dam.

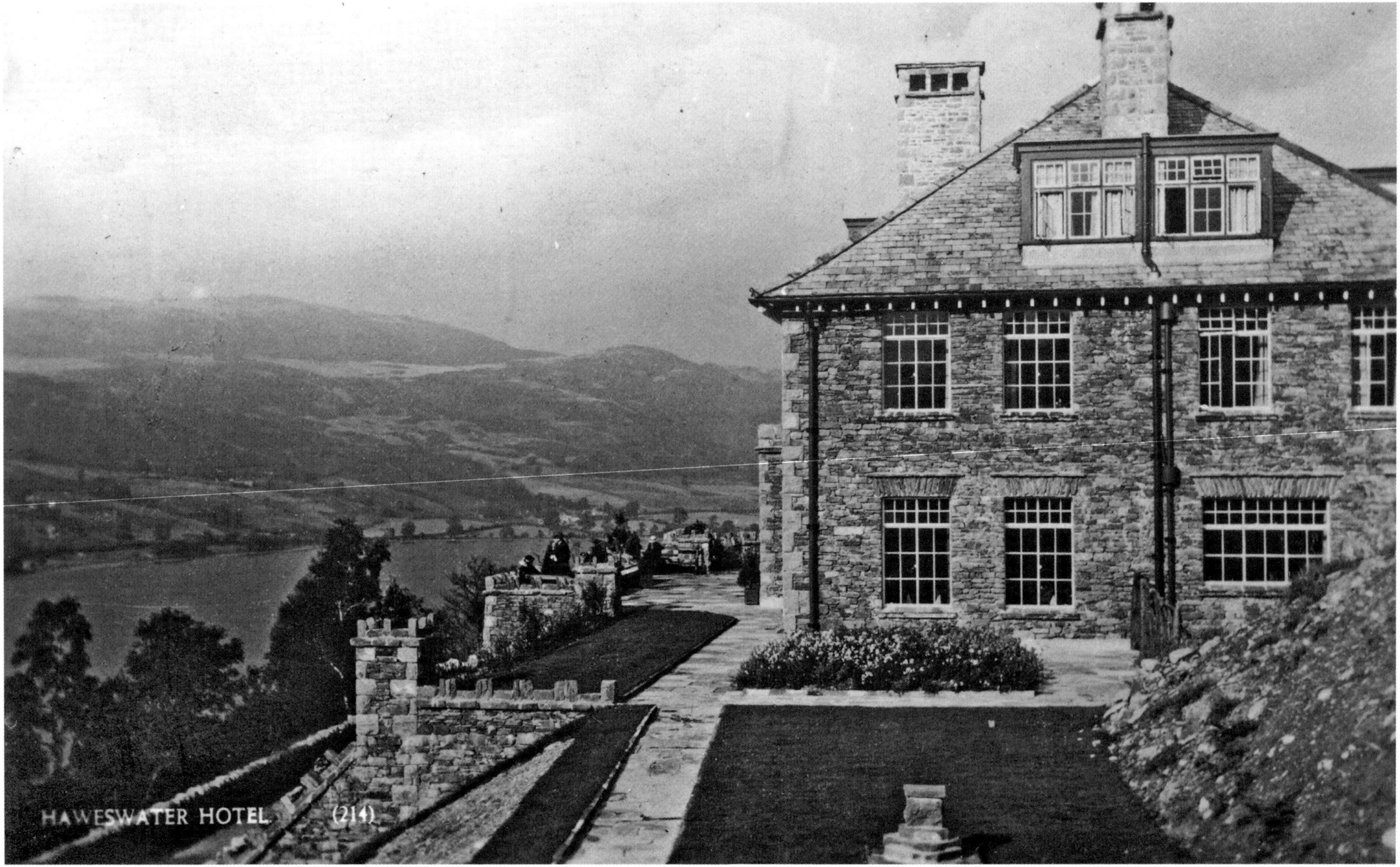

The Haweswater Hotel was constructed by P.A. Baines & Son of Kendal, and the rock gardens were created by a Penrith firm, Herd Bros. The *Herald* reported that the hotel "is the last word in modernity, for it is practically an all-electric hotel and the furnishings and fittings are in keeping with the modern note." The lower floor was very light, with an array of lounges and sun rooms, whilst upstairs there were 14 guest bedrooms, mostly double. The photograph on this page and the one opposite show the hotel and its front terrace, and provide some idea of the views enjoyed by the guests.

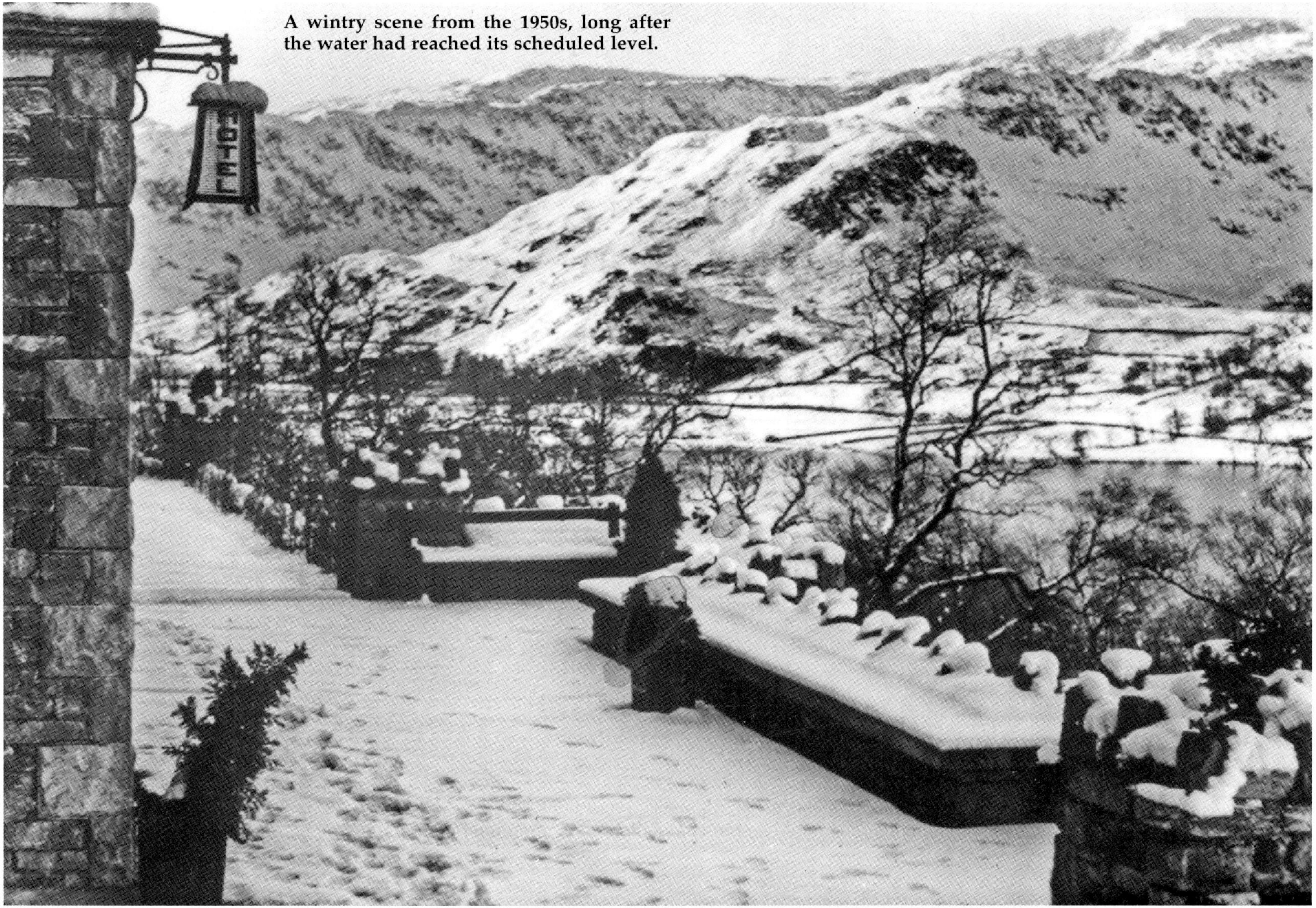

A wintry scene from the 1950s, long after the water had reached its scheduled level.

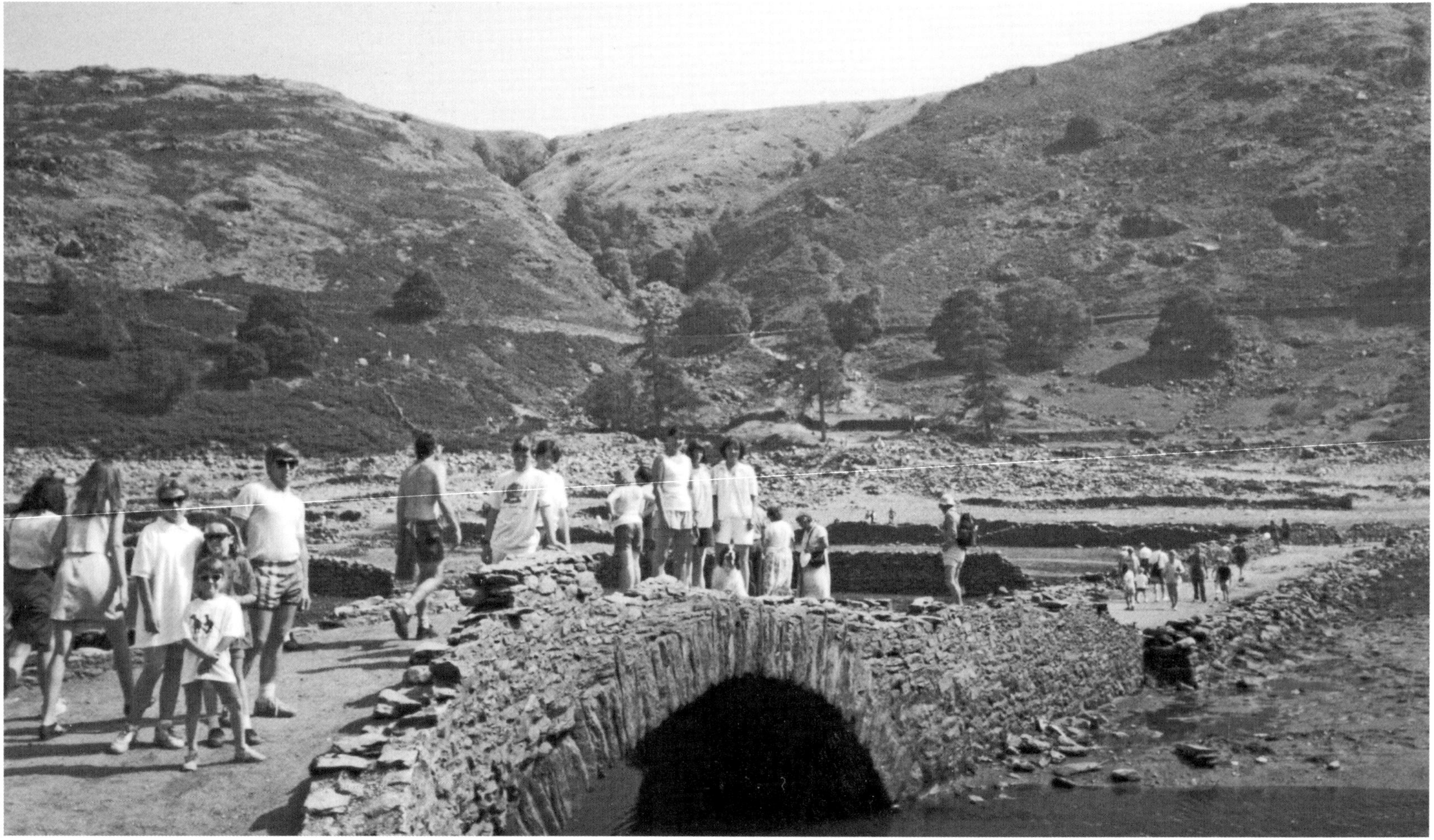

1973 was the first of the "drought years". The water level dropped by over 50 feet and a flood of tourists arrived at the valley to trudge along the muddy lanes and locate the remains of former buildings. The old bridges were still intact, streams ran in their old courses and the Dun Bull's tennis court was easily spotted. The most severe drought of the century came in 1984. By July the water level was falling by about three feet a week and there was a national fascination with Mardale. Former inhabitants were interviewed, ice-cream and burger vans appeared in the valley and the new road was choked by a torrent of sightseers. The police had eventually to close the road. Even then, some people walked miles over the hills to gaze at the exposed ruins of the former settlement.